A SPACIOUS LIFE

TRADING HUSTLE AND HURRY FOR THE GOODNESS OF LIMITS

ASHLEY HALES

An imprint of InterVarsity Press
Downers Grove, Illinois

InterVarsity Press
P.O. Box 1400, Downers Grove, IL 60515-1426
ivpress.com
email@ivpress.com

InterVarsity Press® is the book-publishing division of InterVarsity Christian Fellowship/USA®, a movement of students and faculty active on campus at hundreds of universities, colleges, and schools of nursing in the United States of America, and a member movement of the International Fellowship of Evangelical Students. For information about local and regional activities, visit intervarsity.org.

Scripture quotations, unless otherwise noted, are from The Holy Bible, English Standard Version, copyright © 2001 by Crossway Bibles, a division of Good News Publishers. Used by permission. All rights reserved.

While any stories in this book are true, some names and identifying information may have been changed to protect the privacy of individuals.

Published in association with the literary agent Don Gates of The Gates Group, www.the-gates-group.com.

The publisher cannot verify the accuracy or functionality of website URLs used in this book beyond the date of publication.

Cover design and image composite: David Fassett
Interior design: Daniel van Loon
Image: window curtain at sunrise: © xijian / iStock / Getty Images Plus

ISBN 978-0-8308-4738-9 (print)
ISBN 978-0-8308-4739-6 (digital)

Printed in the United States of America ∞

InterVarsity Press is committed to ecological stewardship and to the conservation of natural resources in all our operations. This book was printed using sustainably sourced paper.

Library of Congress Cataloging-in-Publication Data
A catalog record for this book is available from the Library of Congress.

P 23 22 21 20 19 18 17 16 15 14 13 12 11 10 9 8 7 6 5 4 3 2 1
Y 41 40 39 38 37 36 35 34 33 32 31 30 29 28 27 26 25 24 23 22 21

"Every now and then, it's helpful to be reminded of how un-American the gospel is. The gospel is not *anti*-American because Jesus is for people from every nation, tribe, and tongue, but it is un-American because Jesus does not call us to an endless pursuit of upward mobility, star power, or 'more' as much as to a life of holiness, faithfulness, and rest. If you are weary from the pressure of limitless expectations and you desire healthier rhythms, Ashley has provided an excellent road map."

Scott Sauls, senior pastor of Christ Presbyterian Church in Nashville, Tennessee, and author of *Jesus Outside the Lines*

"From limitations to flourishing, Ashley Hales takes us by the hand and walks us forward into a new freedom that is really an old freedom. She offers the good news that the good life is not what we expected, but it's right here in front of us, waiting between the boundary lines of our limitations. *A Spacious Life* is a welcoming invitation to consider that a smaller life means bigger love."

Sandra McCracken, singer-songwriter and recording artist

"In this wonderfully meditative book, author Ashley Hales rescues us from the siren seduction of self-help. Her vision of the spacious life isn't something to chase after but receive. It's a life modeled by Jesus—a sacramental, attentive, inescapably human life. If you're running breathless, *A Spacious Life* will help you slow down, look up—and breathe."

Jen Pollock Michel, author of *A Habit Called Faith* and *Surprised by Paradox*

"Ashley's words awaken us to our present, particular lives, where showing up needy is our most important work. Here we taste and see and feel the wind on our faces. 'Love exposes us,' Ashley writes. This book is an invitation to that sort of love, a road map for finding our way home."

Shannan Martin, author of *The Ministry of Ordinary Places* and *Falling Free*

"A spacious life is an integrated life, and Ashley Hales has woven together the forms an integrated life takes. From the physical to the spiritual to the emotional to the intellectual, Ashley intersects all the aspects of our humanness, our limitations, to show us how submitting to the skin in which we live can lead us to greener pastures than we imagined."

Lore Ferguson Wilbert, author of *Handle with Care: How Jesus Redeems the Power of Touch in Life and Ministry*

"Nearly every other voice in our culture calls us to defy and detest limits, which is why it is so important for us to understand the different ways proper limits are not only good but essential to human flourishing. Dr. Ashley Hales has written a welcoming, biblically rich, and well-researched book that invites us to live a spacious life. Her painfully relatable stories of life in the contemporary world are paired with insightful cultural analysis, scriptural wisdom, and beautiful prayers to help readers see the goodness in embracing God-given limitations."

Alan Noble, editor in chief of Christ and Pop Culture and assistant professor of English at Oklahoma Baptist University

"Our world tells us to repent of weaknesses and die to limitations because limitations assume a kind of weakness we'd rather not admit. We often assume you can make a lot of money, spend a hundred hours a week at work (because you are needed and important), exercise five days a week, eat extravagant food at extravagant restaurants, look great, have a great sex life and marriage and cute kids, travel extensively, own a great home or apartment—all of it, of course, posted on Instagram. Ashley Hales teaches us that following Jesus is a life of embracing limitations and boasting in weakness. This isn't a disappointing life, it's a better life."

John Starke, lead pastor of Apostles Church Uptown, New York City

"God created limits, and he called them good. That is the message of this book, and it is an urgent word for our overwhelmed, overextended culture. With tenderness, wisdom, and scriptural insight into our times, Ashley Hales has written a spiritual meal of a book. It is lovely and deep and true, and a long overdue invitation to our souls."

Sharon Hodde Miller, author of *Free of Me: Why Life Is Better When It's Not about You*

"We hurry through life, militating against our limits, strictures, and guardrails, yet we find ourselves miserable and exhausted. We kick off constraints, doing whatever we want, all in the name of freedom, and remain deeply dissatisfied. Joy and contentment elude us. In *A Spacious Life*, Ashley Hales draws us to ancient truths: it's within our limits, the life that God has given us, that we flourish. Trying to escape our humanity to be superhuman, unfettered and unencumbered by the quotidian, leads to destruction. Hales, in her inimitable way, deftly and wisely details the path to a spacious life. It is the way of Jesus, the way of wisdom. The way for us. This book hospitably offers an invitation to that sort of life. May we receive it."

Marlena Graves, author of *The Way Up Is Down*

"In our world crowded with schedules, endless lists, and hustle, Hales maps out a way to breathe again. *A Spacious Life* is exactly what I needed. We all need the gentle reminder that our limits are what lead us to real life."

Anjuli Paschall, founder of The Moms We Love Club and author of *Stay: Discovering Grace, Freedom, and Wholeness Where You Never Imagined Looking*

"In this book, Ashley offers us a glimpse of the steady beauty that a small life can provide. Interspersed with descriptions of everyday beauty that we so often overlook, she invites us to slow down and savor the fullness of Christ manifested in every moment. She invites us to find respite from the noisy, squawking world that so often distracts us—to find rest (and purpose) in Jesus. Reading her writing is a wonderful first step to the restfulness of which she speaks. It is a balm for a weary soul."

Jasmine Holmes, author of *Mother to Son*

"Most of us in the West are trying to do too much. We wear ourselves out with our mad dash to make something of ourselves and secure a sense of significance. In *A Spacious Life*, Ashley Hales shows us a better path of flourishing by meditating on the goodness of creaturely limits and the wise way of Jesus. Her theologically rich and pastoral invitation to slow down is a needed tonic in our culture of ambition and excess."

Tish Harrison Warren, Anglican priest and author of *Liturgy of the Ordinary* and *Prayer in the Night*

TO JASON AND KARLA REED,

thank you for creating for us

a spacious place in the turning world.

The lines have fallen for me in pleasant places.

"It seems, then," said Tirian, smiling himself,
"that the Stable seen from within and the Stable
seen from without are two different places."

"Yes," said the Lord Digory. "Its inside
is bigger than its outside."

"Yes," said Queen Lucy. "In our world too,
a Stable once had something inside it that
was bigger than our whole world."

C. S. LEWIS, *THE LAST BATTLE*

He brought me out into a spacious place;
he rescued me because he delighted in me.

PSALM 18:19 (NIV)

CONTENTS

1

THE SUPERMARKET OF LIFE

*An Invitation to Reconsider
Freedom and Significance*

*m*y husband and I lived three glorious years in Edinburgh, Scotland—full of waning northerly light, ancient streets and castles, milky tea, hours spent among old books, and the sense that a full life was finally underway. We were poised between worlds—between the country we were from and the country in which we lived, between college and the fulfilling careers we imagined, newly married but not yet settled down or with children. We'd spend Friday nights bantering with other international grad school students; we watched American TV on DVD; we hosted twenty-five people for an American Thanksgiving and jumped into the rhythms of our parish in the Church of Scotland. Though our meals were often simple, our choices few, it felt like the good life—or at least the beginning of the good life.

There would be time for proper jobs—my husband was training for the pastorate, and I was getting my PhD—and I imagined life a beautiful symphony of ideas. Maybe we'd start a church in Edinburgh, or maybe somewhere else. Maybe I'd get hired to do a postdoctoral fellowship in Europe. Children might come and we'd slot them into a world of poetry, travel, and the life-changing significance of gospel ministry. All was possible.

Yet, when we found ourselves back in Pasadena for work (on the same block we'd lived on three years prior), then a few months later found ourselves expecting our first child, the possibilities narrowed—our lives looked nothing like my rosy-colored, outwardly stretching ideal.

I imagined we could fit our children into the life we had, as if I could file them into one of those black metal tiered inboxes, so that all my early goals—travel, adventure, intellectual pursuits, time to sit in quiet with a cup of tea or to ponder a painting—would not be disturbed. My file-folder life would expand but essentially remain untouched.

What I didn't know, at least not then in a deep-in-your-bones sort of way, was that these limitations on my time, body, and affections were actually an invitation. Instead, I fought them.

For years I fought God about the gap between my imagined life and my given one. My crash course in acknowledging my limits was parenthood. But it seems that God uses many things—a failed job, an angst you can't shake in middle age, a move, a rift in a friendship—to show us our limits. It's easy to take a nostalgic look backward: surely I'd left the good life back in a world of dreams around Edinburgh Castle. Now I was stuck in a hazy world of infant spit-up, a dissertation to finish writing, and no clear sense of God's calling.

Where had the good life gone? Where had *I* gone? Sometimes I railed at God about why the options had dried up, but more often I just ignored him. I'd go to church but not read my Bible; my perfunctory prayers were more out of duty than interest in God's response. I felt constrained, boxed into a new role. I was tethered to people, to a place, to new responsibilities, to a child who needed feeding every three hours. This surely didn't feel like freedom.

It felt like a very small circle in which to move. I wanted big circles, grand vistas, and a life that went up and to the right.

I wish someone had told me to begin to pay careful attention to my limits—that there was a spacious life in there too. That God could be found in the small mustard seed and grain of wheat as well as the sublime sunset or lengthy quiet time. Or maybe they did—and perhaps this is the journey out of youth and into adulthood that we each take—but the only way I could conceive of transformation was with careers and titles, passports and ideas.

• • •

Several years into parenthood an average evening might look like this: I kick the dishwasher closed with a baby strapped to me, all while trying to stir the spaghetti sauce. Having had little adult interaction, I'm hungry to hear about my husband's day and the delightful cacophony of ideas he's had, so I do my best to carry on a coherent conversation amid the cooking and tidying up (maybe we could even have a glass of wine and listen to some music?). Then, a toddler comes into the kitchen, tears and snot running down his face because a toy has gone missing, or he's been asked to help and he doesn't want to, or it's too cold or too hot and he can't find his artistic creation which I thought was just a cardboard box and is now at the bottom of the recycling.

I respond to the urgent. I redirect. I try to extend the grace that I am jealous of, but my anger bubbles. I am tired of always giving. I want control. The pasta water boils over. The moment of conversation is gone, and I realize I simply cannot do it all.

This leads me into a lovely little shame spiral. If I don't just blame my circumstances or anyone within striking distance (tactic one), I think the problem isn't with my life but with how I've ordered it (tactic two). I vow to try harder, get a new dinner routine, and find a new parenting book. And if that doesn't work, I'll sit in my shame, concluding I'm not worth it (tactic three). A mantra of "you do you" doesn't solve shame or loneliness.

I'm not alone. We imagine the shape of the good life as one with endless opportunities from which to choose. But under the heavy burden of "having it all," women, particularly in their thirties to fifties, are feeling the weight.

Ada Calhoun writes of this "experiment in crafting a higher-achieving, more fulfilled, more well-rounded version of the American woman." For women entering middle age, that "experiment" has brought on higher debt and increased pressure with work and family life. Throw in fluctuating hormones in midlife, and the results are more exhaustion, anxiety, depression, and sleeplessness. This is why Calhoun writes that by midlife, many of us "find the experiment is largely a failure." Not only is the experiment a failure but we believe we are too. We've failed by not meeting our ideals, and we've also failed by being deeply unhappy.

If we say the good life is a happy one, and what makes a person happy is freedom, and we define freedom as unlimited autonomy, then all our unlimited autonomy should create happy, contented people. But our unlimited autonomy isn't bringing happiness; it's producing stasis, exhaustion, and hurry. David Brooks says it like this:

> In a culture of "I'm Free to Be Myself," individuals are lonely and loosely attached. Community is attenuated, connections are dissolved, and loneliness spreads. This situation makes it difficult to be good—to fulfill the deep human desires for love and connection. It's hard on people of all ages, but it's especially hard on young adults. They are thrown into a world that is unstructured and uncertain, with few authorities or guardrails except those they are expected to build on their own.

Our freedom narrative in the West—choosing your own destiny according to your own sense of autonomous freedom— is leaving us at sea in endless choice. We are lonely, exhausted, and unsure what success or joy even looks like anymore.

• • •

Does this sound familiar? If you're anxious and feel like you're always on a treadmill of hustle and hurry, I want to bring you along with me to the grocery store—specifically, to an American grocery store after our years in Scotland.

Not having had a car during our years in Edinburgh, we'd pop into the grocery store almost every day and carry our groceries home. We'd run down to a corner shop when the food staples ran out. We'd learned to make sure we had our Monday meal prep done by Saturday, since by Sunday, the stores were likely low on milk and bread (and the shops closed early).

When we walked into a large American grocery store after years away, I stopped, taking in the wide, shiny aisles. There were a hundred varieties of Cheerios and granola, half of them tagged with red sale tickets. I remember staring blankly at the condiments. There was avocado oil mayo, vegan mayo, regular full-fat mayo, fat-free mayo, off-brand mayo, and a hundred other permutations in every size imaginable. Why did we need a thousand options and two aisles for condiments? I dropped my basket and went home. It was simply too much. I couldn't choose.

When every option is available to us, we don't actually have freedom; we tend to shut down. I experienced what sociologists call choice overload (or paralysis) and decision fatigue. If you've ever tried to pick out a paint color for a wall, stood in your closet full of clothes with "nothing to wear," or found yourself trying to find the right word at the end of the day but your head is muddled from the thousands of decisions you've already sifted through, you know this doesn't feel like freedom. Like too many condiments to choose from, we don't need more choices to live the good life. We probably need less. We need instructions, a guide, and appropriately placed guardrails to show us the way forward.

The American grocery store—along with images of success like "climbing ladders"—showed me how I'd made the good life a cocktail of endless personal choice, ambition, and hurry. I'd shaken them all up and added Jesus as a cherry on top. The answer to this overwhelm wasn't that I simply needed a change of circumstances (like another brand of condiment) to make me happy.

The problem of my satisfaction didn't in fact rest on a curated life I could create from the ground up, where the issue was that all the stuff of life—relationships, work, my husband's career, the continent we lived on—got in the way.

The problem wasn't that I had to manage my time better, do more, or work harder to get what I wanted.

I had to upend my idea of the good life; the good life wasn't found in my power to choose whatever I wanted.

Jesus could not be a garnish on top of my unlimited autonomy. He was the gentle shepherd leading in the narrow way. The way into a more spacious life was through a doorway I didn't want to enter: right through my limits.

• • •

The gospel is the good news that Jesus' life, death, resurrection, and ascension accomplish for us what hustle and hurry never can. We do not have to push past limits to earn our perfection before a holy God; instead, God comes near, taking on our human limits to bring us into relationship with himself. When we place our trust in him, he exchanges our sin and shame for his beloved perfection. But how do we

> The gospel is the good news that Jesus' life, death, resurrection, and ascension accomplish for us what hustle and hurry never can.

get that goodness in us? It starts by walking out of the grocery store, stepping down from the ladder, and replanting ourselves in this better story.

Whether or not we call ourselves Christians, most of us do not practically live out this better story, the one lived under the rule and leading of Jesus. The good news of Jesus takes a stick of dynamite to our carefully ordered, autonomous lives on the right and the left, so that we're forced to reckon with this reminder from Fleming Rutledge: "If the kingdom of heaven is at hand, as John the Baptist says, then all our other kingdoms are called radically into question, including my own private kingdom, and yours." We are not the monarchs of our own lives.

Freedom is not simply freedom *from* constraints but *for* something—for love. Jesus models for us what this freedom for the sake of love looks like: for those who come weary and worn to Jesus, it looks like healing. It tastes like bread in hungry bellies and brings a justice and peace deeper than what a full bank account could offer. The freedom Jesus holds out is an entrance into something more beautiful than simply being turned loose in the condiment aisle or asked to curate our own lives. Limits are good.

> Freedom is not simply freedom *from* constraints but *for* something—for love.

Wait, I can hear you asking, limits are . . . *good*, full stop? Like, not just something to push past or knock down? If you're a bit skeptical, perhaps you can relate to a conversation I had with my neighbor who, when I told her limits were good, guffawed: "You mean I don't have be good at it all—building multiple businesses and have them firing on all cylinders, volunteering in my twins' kindergarten class, all while caring for my partner who has just been diagnosed with cancer?" "No, you don't," I told her. "You can be human."

These good, God-given limits are for all people in all times and places, not the sorts of societal limits imposed on others to oppress or silence. As God's creatures made in his image, we are all limited by our bodies, by our personalities, by our places, by our circles of relation, and by those for whom we are responsible. We are limited in our power and authority and by particular seasons of work, health, and faith. We are limited in our time, our attention, and our calling. Our God-given limits are the doorway into a more spacious life.

What might happen if we tried embracing our limits as gifts for our flourishing rather than barriers to our success? I think we'd find we were beginning to walk in the way of Jesus.

But what does this look like? It looks like love and feels just as disorienting. The missiologist Lesslie Newbigin wrote: "True freedom is not found by seeking to develop the powers of the self without limits, for the human person is

> Our God-given limits are the doorway into a more spacious life.

not made for autonomy but for true relatedness in love and obedience; and this also entails the acceptance of limits as a necessary part of what it means to be human." Limits remind us we are but dust. Limits remind us too that we are made in God's image, "lower than the angels," the fragile and glorious crown of creation (Heb 2:7). We are made by Love for love, and love joyfully accepts constraints in order to love others particularly and fully.

If you're a bit like Augustine, that patron saint of restless souls, and you're realizing that "the loss of guardrails only meant ending up in the ditch, [and] you start to wonder whether freedom is all it's cracked up to be—or whether freedom might be something other than the absence of constraint and the multiplication of options," I invite you along for the journey.

The doorway feels a little tight at first, but if today you're burned out from hurry and hustle, or you find yourself crushed under the weight of the "free" identity you must endlessly create, may I offer you another way? There is a spacious life waiting for you inside the narrow gate.

As we go on this journey together, we will follow the only person who is both perfect and limited, Jesus. As fully God and fully human, Jesus shows us how to embrace our limits under the loving reign of God, condescending as he does to leave heavenly glory to come to his creation as a human. All aspects of his coming—from his birth to his death and resurrection— were acts of particular love. Each chapter of this book moves deeper into this story, holding out an invitation to us from the life of Christ. Each offers a new way of seeing so we might begin to imagine how our own stories map onto the story of Jesus.

Each chapter also ends with a short prayer—a way to practice being with Jesus in the limits of your time, even as you read. If prayer is new for you, try these on for size. Take these with you into your hearts, homes, small groups, and churches as starting points.

Duck your head and walk through the narrow gate. Jesus is not only our good shepherd leading the way to an abundant life, but he is also the gate: "I am the gate; whoever enters through me will be saved. They will come in and go out, and find pasture" (Jn 10:9 NIV). Just beyond is that pastureland you seek. Join me for a journey into internal landscapes. Here is a more spacious life.

2

AND LIMITS WERE GOOD, VERY GOOD

An Invitation to Smallness

*O*ne long weekend we took our children to Los Angeles, to the hills under the Hollywood sign, to Griffith Observatory. The air was clear, the observatory a stark white nestled in green hills. It felt iconic: the city that isn't quite a city lay below us, but from high up we could make Los Angeles what we wanted it to be.

We settled into our seats with our chairs leaned back to see the show on the domed screen. The room darkened. Constellations danced across the ceiling. We learned how ancient peoples navigated by the stars and worshiped them, and how we are but a small part of a small galaxy and that there are at least one hundred billion galaxies beyond in such a vast expanse. The film zoomed in to Los Angeles, to Griffith Observatory, where we were, and then zoomed out, and zoomed out, and zoomed out—and we were lost in space—in galaxies unknown.

I couldn't imagine how big God must be to have thought this all up and then made it so. We wiggled a bit uncomfortably in our seats. For we are very small.

• • •

The world came to be with boundary lines. These boundary lines—these limits—create order for creation to flourish. Limits show us how the world works best. First there was nothing, and then through the powerful word of the Creator, it became something—named, identified, given purpose and meaning—at the will and authority of the God who is beyond space and time.

The breath of God spoke binding words, vows of who he was and is, and what and who creation would be. From an utterance of "let there be light," suddenly light was separated from darkness. Waters were separated from an expanse he named heaven. The earth sprouted vegetation: seeds multiplied in accordance with their own kind, trees according to their own kind. The seas teemed with creatures of the deep, and the land grew with living creatures—each producing within the lines and limits of God's own choosing. Each fulfilling its purpose. It was good.

And God got intimate, his hands in the mess of things— down in the dirt. He planted a garden in Eden, scattering seeds like a sower, creating a home with boundary lines for the crown glory of creation: humanity, the image of God himself in male and female form. He planted pleasant, shady trees, a delight to the eyes with their vibrant colors and juicy fruit. Oh, it was good.

And within that place, God took dirt from the ground and formed a human; God breathed into his nostrils and he became alive with the very breath of life. And when no helper was found suitable for him, God formed a woman, bone of Adam's bones and flesh of Adam's flesh. The two were to be one flesh, unashamed, caretakers of Eden. It was very good.

Creation was given limits: to reproduce, to be subject to the changing of seasons. Subject to time, change, and a cycle between fallow and flourishing. There were limits on celestial bodies: the sun was to rule the day and the moon the night. Even the naming of the world, of light and dark, of seas and land, gave assignments and limits to creation. Planets were not to go just anywhere but had an orbit; vegetation grew according to the limits of its seasons, and animals flourished best within a limited habitat. Without the loving setting of limits on the natural world, it would be void and without form.

Limits are built into the fabric of creation as part of God's loving rule and care. Limits are not a result of sin, strictures to hold us down, but a part of God's very good plan. Limits create for us a home; they create the condition for flourishing.

Limits, given to the world by a loving God, are the conditions for life.

We are no different. People too were given limits not to restrict and cajole, but like all of creation, for their flourishing. Adam and Eve were limited to a place. Eden, their home, was to be where they lived out the faithfulness of their union for the good stewarding of all creation. As the crown of creation, they wielded power and authority as stewards, but within the loving rule of the Creator of the cosmos. They were to care for creation, to name animals, to have vegetation for food. There were also limitations of what not to do: they were not to eat from the tree of the knowledge of good and evil.

> Limits, given to the world by a loving God, are the conditions for life.

Adam and Eve were given to each other only to live within the limits of a covenant: a binding relationship proceeding from God that fostered trust, care, and offspring. Limits create the conditions for relationship—they provide the guardrails to guide us to the place where we know and are known. These vows protect.

Everything had a place, a role. There was an order and authority under which humanity sat and a ceiling to their autonomy, and there was an invitation to responsibly care for others and for their particular spot of land. Limits were very good—they showed the path for the world as it ought to be.

Limits of relationship, limits of purpose and calling, limits of authority—each was an invitation into community with one another and with their Creator who walked with them in the cool of the evening.

Limits were an invitation into flourishing. But all that changed.

• • •

Everything was given to Adam and Eve for food: the blueberries for picking, the basil for plucking, the vines for tending. Yet one tree was encircled with a no: the tree of the knowledge of good and evil. If they disobeyed this limit, death would be the result.

In a slithering sort of question, the serpent asked Eve: "Did God actually say, 'You shall not eat of any tree in the garden'?" (Gen 3:1). The serpent asked. Eve responded. And from that moment on, all of humanity followed in the lineage of the treacherous disavowal of God as king. We disbelieved his goodness.

We began to believe the good life is a life without limits. More fruit, more knowledge, more suspicion, more work, and more on our to-do lists to try to earn for ourselves the things we had already been given: a name, a relationship, a life, a purpose.

And in the scene that followed, limits were no longer for flourishing. After the fall of our first parents, boundaries were something to push past, to transgress. It's worth pausing to note how we use the word *transgression* for "sin." With its Latin roots, "across" and "go," to transgress means to exceed proper limits. Our first parents crossed over, transgressed, as they moved from seeing God's good limits as the conditions for life to seeing them as barriers to human freedom.

I love how the early church father Athanasius writes of why God enters into his creation: "It was our sorry case that caused the Word to come down, our transgression that called out His love for us, so that He made haste to help us and to appear among us."

God, like a parent sensing his precious children are in dire danger, picks up his skirts, so to speak, his hands still wet from dishwashing and cooking, to save his children. He cares not about his appearance or what it looks like from the outside, disheveled and in disarray. He is intent on his purpose—to save, to bring his children home. He crosses over to bring us back. It is our sorry state that fomented the very heart of God to do something about us. Love saves. Love doesn't care what it looks like.

What we need is a loving parent to scoop us up from playground politics, brush us off, wrap their arms around us, and bring us home.

That is why the eternal Word came. That is why the Word became flesh.

• • •

It's hard to think of Jesus, the eternal Word, present at the creation of the world, preexistent before there was a cosmos to even marvel at, squeezing through a young woman's birth canal. God became human. The magnitude of God's rescue plan happened small, through the birth of a baby. Jesus welcomed small—he welcomed limits—as the pathway to love.

The promised Messiah, whose voice sounds like rushing waters, who holds the key to death and Hades, also grew in secret in Mary's womb. He kicked and elbowed as all babies do, and came at the appointed time, though I'm sure it didn't seem right to Mary and Joseph.

> Jesus welcomed small—he welcomed limits—as the pathway to love.

I imagine Mary breathed through the contractions, giving herself to the process of her own opening body, with the same acceptance that she had told the angel: "May it be to me as you say." *May it be as you say.* These are not the words of inaction or self-obliteration; they are words of acceptance; they are vows. They are words that create a place.

So, Mary bore down, grabbing on to Joseph, wondering, even as she submitted herself to wave after wave of contraction: *Is this how the Son of God comes? Here, now, like this?*

The master of the universe submitted to become multiplying cells, submitted to the slow process of growth in a human womb. Before that, he orchestrated and waited, through generation upon generation of prophecy, babies born, and his people falling away. Finally he was born in the city of King David; he had the vernix scrubbed off him and his umbilical cord cut, and the air of the earth filled his lungs. All this shows us how Love flourishes by limits. He cried a cry to let everyone know he had arrived: *I'm here. Finally. The rescue all humanity has been waiting for.*

• • •

We shift in our seats uncomfortably. If God became human—if he's really, truly here—what does that mean for us? The second person of the Trinity became small. A more spacious life is not to be gained by becoming bigger or by spreading out more thinly; it's by following the way of Jesus. We too must reckon with our smallness.

We try to be big. We ignore the needs of the body. We drink too much coffee and skimp on sleep. We measure our worth on our social media feeds or by a number in the bank or on a scale. We have transgressed the limits of our attention and care: cramming too much in our calendars, walking past our family and neighbors in favor of what we have set out to accomplish.

When I've gone past God-given limits—choosing instead to try to earn through hustle what I've already been given, the gracious care of God—I end up weary, overwhelmed, confused, and discontented.

Hustle and hurry are not just what we do: they have become states of the soul. When we can effectively opt in or out (like plugging in technology) to any form of community (in person or virtual), any place, any job, any spouse, or almost any body, we are not free. When every option is open to us, we are trapped in our so-called freedom. We are crushed under the pressure of trying to be God: to create—at every moment—a state of happiness.

When we live our lives by the story of unlimitedness, we believe small equals powerless. Not wanting to lose control, if we have the resources and personality, we puff ourselves up like an exotic bird pulling out the stops to attract attention. It's a dance that's ridiculous, but we seem to know no other way. Or we slink back into the shadows, become a target for exploitation and find ourselves in a vortex of shame that cuts us off from others.

But what if the guardrails of love drew us to find our proper place—not exploited, not stepping on others to make our significance known? Jesus dignifies the ordinary, material world. Perhaps because he simply didn't need to clothe himself in the forms of worldly ambition or power, Jesus chose to enter small—through the womb of a young girl, with shepherds and animals as his attendants.

He shows us how in the story of God, small things are valuable and effective. Might recovering our limits help us to recover our common humanity?

We are the created ones, under the power and authority of an unlimited God. God's power expresses itself in self-limiting and self-giving love, not in an exploitative power. So, as we meditate on how the incarnate Christ willingly took on our limits because of love, we see our limited humanity as something to be embraced. Something both cherished and needing rescue.

A small, practical step toward embracing a more spacious life is to recognize that we are human: bodies, souls, minds, with natural limits. You might need nine hours of sleep and hate Brussels sprouts. You may have an autoimmune disease that limits your energy and what you can do. You may be tall or short, large or small, extroverted or introverted, with a shade of skin unlike your neighbor's.

Bottom line: if the second person of the Trinity took on flesh, then all your particularities matter. Your limits create a unique path whereby Jesus comes to you in this moment and invites you to live for the life of the world.

Jesus invites us to see our bodies as good, the material world as part of God's kingdom. If the gates of hell cannot prevail against God's kingdom, our limits are not barriers that God cannot work through. Our limits, rather, invite us into a proper relationship with God.

> Your limits create a unique path whereby Jesus comes to you in this moment and invites you to live for the life of the world.

Here we remember ourselves as we are: beloved children. In God's kingdom, small is a gift.

We are invited to name our limits with God. We bring them to our unlimited God and ask he would work in and through them. I practice thanking him for my local life (even as I struggle with wanderlust), for the ways that the limits of ministry have helped me love Jesus and his church even when I didn't feel like it. My biggest growth point in parenting is realizing that though it has narrowed my "free" time, attention, and availability, it has also helped me to grow in empathy, to practice asking for forgiveness, and it reminds me I cannot meet everyone's needs. This is a gift.

A "do more" life drains us of energy, compassion, mission, and peace. The magazines and self-help books tell us this is the good life, but the kingdom of God says otherwise. The kingdom of God is a net, a pearl of great price. It is yeast, a hidden treasure, small as a mustard seed. These are small, limited things created to do something: to feed, to create beauty, to transform ordinary elements into what they are supposed to be. To get this spacious life in us, we start by reckoning with our own designed smallness and thanking God for it. Jesus embraces the small and dignifies it.

We are invited to practice being small. We are invited to name our limits—the ones we feel and the ones we don't, to ask for eyes to see the limits we're blind to.

Eugene Peterson's paraphrase of Jesus' words in Matthew's Gospel are an invitation to all of us:

> Are you tired? Worn out? Burned out on religion? Come to me. Get away with me and you'll recover your life. I'll show you how to take a real rest. Walk with me and work with me—watch how I do it. Learn the unforced rhythms of grace. I won't lay anything heavy or ill-fitting on you. Keep company with me and you'll learn to live freely and lightly. (Mt 11:28-30 *The Message*)

On the threshold of a more spacious life, will you keep coming back here: laying down hustle and hurry for the wide expanse of "the unforced rhythms of grace"?

A more spacious life always starts and ends with grace, with the strong and powerful vows spoken into the fabric of creation and woven through the life of Jesus. And so I'll leave you, my dear readers, with a little prayer: the hesitant words of an uttered yes to this spacious life that looks small and homely from the outside. Even still, we choose to pin our audacious hopes that the inside is bigger than the outside, that there are worlds upon worlds in the smallness.

• • •

Triune God who is both entirely other and also intimate,

I can't imagine my way into the incarnation. My mind and comprehension are small. What I do know is my anxiety, my overwhelm, and the way talk of "the good life" presses in from each side. I'm worn out with hurry, and I speak about hustle with the language of virtue. Forgive me for going beyond the limits you intend for me.

Give me courage, Jesus, to find my deepest identity in you—to practice naming my limits and giving them to you.

I'm opening the door to the small and faithful story of God. I'm afraid: What am I doing? Will I be swallowed up, spit out, or made invisible?

Yet here we go! Spirit, comfort me, direct my steps.

Amen.

3

JESUS ISN'T ON INSTAGRAM

An Invitation to Set Aside Social Media

i turn away, I don't want to be presumed staring. But I like watching the older woman reading, chewing her sandwich, and sipping her coffee in the corner of the cafe. I like the blue lines on the backs of her hands, how she's content in her ball cap and unremarkable sneakers. That even her casual outfit needn't be put together with rips in her jeans in all the right places and the tennis shoe that shows she's put together but not too formal. I like how her pinky finger curves in to touch her ring finger, that she rests her hand on her chin when she reads. I like how she holds the sandwich like a sandwich ought to be held—perhaps unthinkingly, or maybe with the utmost care—but definitely not in a way to focus on herself, how she looks or what might be an Instagrammable moment.

I like that she seems at home in herself and seems to know how to inhabit this moment in time. And there's not a hint of digital intrusion or posturing. (I blush. I've just taken a photo of my teapot and fancy theology books.) When she gets up, she leaves her recycled napkin crumpled up in her porcelain cup.

Is this how life once was?

• • •

If the doorway to a more spacious life is an invitation to smallness, once we enter, we quickly feel the limits of our humanity. We exist as bodies in time with blue-veined hands and age spots. Yet, we try to push past, *transgress*, these limits. One way we do this is through habits of hurry. It's not just our constant physical movement that keeps us hurried but also our habits of digital consumption have us trying to be in all places at once. Online we can pretend to be everywhere: in and out of conversations, amassing swathes of knowledge, commenting, liking, and retweeting.

We use our phones to push off the limits of our bodies and places—and we're addicted to them.

There are now support groups for smartphone addiction. The average person looks at their phone eighty times a day and spends an average of three hours daily on their phone. Our to-do lists are punctuated to check email; our conversations are interrupted to respond to people who aren't in front of us. Our hearts and imaginations are caught by the news headlines rather than our neighbors. Our digital diet is turned into self-directed messages of shame: envy creeps in when we view someone else's vacation photos, a video of their fun parenting makes us feel inferior, political commentary makes us heated, debate on Twitter takes away time from the slower work of face-to-face connection and reconciliation.

Social media addiction also changes our neurochemistry: our slumped posture produces cortisol; the backlit phone and blue light can suppress melatonin (needed for sleep); and a recent study with "hard-core gamers showed gray-matter atrophy in the right orbitofrontal cortex, bilateral insula, and right supplementary-motor areas of the brain. These parts of the brain are related to impulse control, planning, organization, and even compassion." Our phones are literally changing our bodies, our sleep and stress levels, and our ability to connect empathetically with others.

I try to keep my smartphone from calling the shots so I plug it in in the kitchen; but each time I walk past it, I do a quick refresh of the inbox, a quick skip through social media. I use this digital limb to puff up a pretended omniscience: I do not want to think of myself as limited in my desires, time, and attention.

Marketers know that the best way to mold us into effective consumers is to keep us addicted and coming back for more—for personal validation, updates and statuses, deals and price changes, to peek behind the curtain of fame and popularity.

Addiction isn't just measured in time spent connected to screens but also in how it dulls our spiritual sensibilities. We use social media to blunt the edges of overwhelm, to find something to thrill us, to assert our correctness, to fit in, to feel like we mean something. Lacking digital constraint, we shout our opinions, amass information like it's the source of life, use social media to perform our pain, or alternatively disappear into scrolling. Like Linus's blanket, we hold on to our phones, scrolling to be productive or to soothe our deep fears of failure, our anxieties about the unknown, and to escape the pains of ordinary life and conflict.

It's easier to scroll through Twitter and Instagram than pray. It's easier to distract ourselves from angst through the proliferation of pretty squares. Online we exist in a wide digital expanse, bypassing the limits of our bodies, emotions, places, and time, and it feels freeing, at first.

However, when we're able to keep on creating our own identities via social media, what we end up with isn't freedom— it's slavery. What began as a break from the pangs of life in community has become automatic. More than just a reflex, David Zahl writes about the deeper ways our technology forms us: "We use technology to rebel against anything that would seek to constrain or confine us. To the Law that tells us we are creatures, men and women with limits and dependencies, we shake our fists and insist we are Creators. I can handle things just fine on my own." Even if the good life were found in unfettered freedom (and it's not), we aren't even free by our own definitions. We're chained to our devices, mediating life behind a screen, and trying to push against our common limits of humanity.

More convenience and more virtual connection are not leaving us more satisfied. Though we've never been more connected, our connections are thin. Most of us don't have thick communities; it's why we're dying of loneliness. More freedom and digital space leave us feeling not more free but more claustrophobic.

• • •

When we're on our social media platform of choice, we're often looking for connection and consolation. Life seems simpler in little squares. When we're virtually everywhere at once and yet in no place, we can forget that we are limited, finite, enfleshed, and mortal.

If our sins—even small sins of omission like digital addiction—are really misdirected desires and affections, then our restless scrolling shows our restless hearts. We're little children wandering the aisles of the internet because we've lost the presence of our loving parent. We are desperate for the attention of a good Father who sees us. We have no idea how to rest. It's easier to be everywhere at once online. We turn to the stories our phones hold out for us to tell us who we are. I wonder if the lobbing of intellectual grenades, the picking apart of people by virtual strangers on the internet, are often just misdirected hungry cries of the child: "See me, notice me, know me, love me."

> We're little children wandering the aisles of the internet because we've lost the presence of our loving parent.

Jesus, the Word made flesh, shows us the face of the Father. What we hunger for when we're flitting around online is purpose, meaning, direction, revelation—all things that are ultimately found in the attention of a first-century Jewish man who says, "Whoever has seen me has seen the Father" (Jn 14:9). It is his unhurried attention we crave, his healing touch, his piercing wisdom and upside-down kingdom. Whether it's from shame or fear, we, like our first parents, choose to hide instead. Social media addiction is just one of our modern-day methods to push off the fierce and tender presence of God. But Jesus isn't on Instagram.

. . .

They were poor. We know this because the two young turtledoves Joseph and Mary brought was the smallest offering they were allowed as devout Jews and yet the largest they likely could afford. With two birds, they presented the Incarnate Word on the steps of the temple in Jerusalem. Poor and yet the richest people on the planet. Paradox upon paradox in the person of Jesus: God and man, divine and human, gentle and demanding, servant and king conquering death through death. Though we think of temples as holy and untouchable, ice palaces where only the perfect get in, it was a home too—to two people bent by life: Simeon and Anna.

Each walked in such close step with the Spirit of God that they were directed into a life of perpetual praise and prophecy. Both seemed to show up just in time (not sweeping in with the restless breathing we all do as we rush around) but with the measured pace of listening to the Spirit.

Theirs was a slow life, one lived in the present tense. Simeon, a man who walked with the Spirit, knew God so well that the pathways he traveled were formed by God. As Jesus would be led by the Spirit into the wilderness, Simeon was led into the temple, his spirit testifying to the Spirit's prodding ("yes this is the one") so that he took the infant Christ in his wrinkled arms—the mother of the Messiah and Joseph open-mouthed— and prophesied him to be "a light for revelation to the Gentiles, and for glory to your people Israel" (Lk 2:32).

A light. Glory. All wrapped up in the flesh of a newborn consecrated with a small and poor offering and named "holy to the Lord." But not just light and glory: sorrow and division would be the portion of everyone connected to Jesus too, a life where "sorrow and love flow mingled down." Simeon looked at Mary, prophesying over her that a "sword will pierce through your own soul also" (Lk 2:35).

But at that moment, the poor parents just had a baby and their small offering. Mary was still recovering from birth. Everything was tender. Perhaps on the temple steps Anna met them, brought by the Spirit to witness the Christ. Her own sorrow, her years of widowhood, were transformed into an offering of praise: thanking God that Jerusalem was finally going to be comforted and redeemed.

What she had sown in years of service and love rose to the top. Gratitude bubbled over into proclamation and prophecy. And it happened through years of unhurried presence.

How did people like Simeon and Anna see the baby and understand when so many didn't?

They did not seek grandeur; they sought the presence of God. They knew their place and their limitations: their bodies bent with age, their life events had whittled them down to what was essential so they could find in God blessing and contentment. They were unhurried. They stopped and listened. They paid attention and they knew the Messiah when they saw him.

In the story of grace, the lack of hurry makes room for presence.

In the story of grace, the lack of hurry makes room for presence.

• • •

We have limits of ability. Limits of age, gender, opportunity. We bear generational conflict, mental illness, and addictions. Particular life events shake us, limiting how, when, and where we flourish. We live in places, in houses, with people. Some of us have grief or abuse passed down. Some had passive-aggressive parents, or no parents at all; too much money or not enough. We were given access through status, privilege, race, acclaim, or financial security, or we were denied access.

All these limits form us: they provide the contours of our "one wild and precious life." Some, with limited options, like Mary and Joseph and Anna and Simeon, flourished. Others, like the rich young ruler to whom Jesus later speaks, had worldly acclaim—riches, success, reputation—yet they wither in their excess. A spacious life isn't contingent on privilege. When Jesus told the rich young ruler he lacked one thing and to sell his possessions and give them away, he went away sad. His stuff, like our digital addiction, seemed to provide endless options. This "just a bit more," this vista of supposed endless opportunity, is the siren call of our contemporary freedom narrative.

Jesus invites the young man into a life of kingdom limits, something far greater than the "more" we think will satisfy us. When we note our smallness and creatureliness and cease our addiction to hurry, we are graced with the attention of God.

What if our humanity and all the limits we've been born into could somehow work like a goad to drive us to Jesus?

What if our limits weren't curses but blessings?

Perhaps we look to a screen because it's too painful to remember we are mortal. To sit in our limits and let them wash

Positive bias in problem-solving

over us. To embrace this body, this moment in time, this feeling, or this place.

To remember again how to be a body, I do small things: I take walks so I'm not just what I think and feel. I fill a bath with Epsom salts and enjoy the feel of hot water on my tired feet. I put lotion slowly all over my body, even the squishy parts. I pause in the middle of the day to enjoy a mug of hot tea with a splash of milk. I practice inhabiting a moment, a body, a place, instead of giving in to habits of hurry or digital everywhere-ism.

To enter in to the spacious life, we remember:

We cannot be everywhere at once. When we reach for our phones to quell the ache of being human with our limits of time, attention, love, and desire, we live as if we were God— omniscient and omnipresent. The salve is to embrace good human limits: to practice presence by limiting our desire for vistas of virtual realities. Reminding us to heal from "our disease of limitlessness," Wendell Berry writes: "We will have to start over, with a different and much older premise: the naturalness and, for creatures of limited intelligence, the necessity, of limits." We practice being one person in one place in one moment of time.

Our deepest identity is that we are dear, little children. The call for us cynical and jaded adults is to remember anew that we are

> Living as a child is an invitation, not a shame.

children of Love. Living as a child is an invitation, not a shame. A "get to" instead of something to hide, resent, or feel ashamed and embarrassed by. We *get to* be limited. We get to have bodies, needs, and desires, and our digital consumption cannot give us the presence we crave.

I have a photo of one of my children: on a day of pure sunshine, he is running down the hillside, leading with his chest, his smile and stride wide as his speed picks up. Running is pure delight. Again and again he ran down that hill, feeling the sun kiss his head in early summer, sensing the pleasure of limbs moving at full force. His mama couldn't help but smile too. Here was joy with flesh on. This is what the invitation, the *get to* of being a child with the attention of her Father, feels like.

We have a Father who welcomes us into a present, unhurried life, who accepts our paltry offerings. We have a Father who knows what is best for us, who lovingly cares and shepherds us to embrace our limits, so we can know his love.

We must practice bodily rather than technological rhythms. We must start by putting screens away. We use them to push off dissatisfaction with long lines, the emotional fallout from a fight, boredom, and loneliness. We're being formed by screens instead of through embodied and habitual spiritual practices that move us toward Jesus. It's okay to feel the weight of our overwhelm and ask Jesus to meet us in it rather than ignoring it through technological distraction, or weaponizing our pain for virtual strangers. Could you put down your phone long enough to sit with God in that small place?

We must learn to see our limits as the entrance into the good life, not what bars us from it. Consider how you might enter through a narrow gate by embracing your actual life—your real body, the limits of your place, your family, your age and stage, your finances. Write down your limits. Pray through them.

Are you living under the loving rule and guidance of our good shepherd—the one who lived an unhurried life before the face of his Father—or are you endlessly and exhaustingly feeling the pressure to create for yourself an identity?

Maybe it's time to be a child again.

• • •

Father, I confess I reach for anything to make me feel seen, known, and loved.

Deliver me from the fear of being invisible, unnoticed or uncared for. As I put down my phone, please sit with me in my emotions, my overwhelm, my fear, my anger, my covetousness, and my constant striving to try to make something of myself.

Show me how your guardrails are good. I give you my small offering: even today that is my fear, my questions, my insecurities that I use my phone to try to fix. Create in me the unhurried life.

Amen.

4

OF CUCUMBERS AND
SKIPPING STONES

An Invitation to Wait

*a*s a family, we needed to see something grow, to learn to care for green and growing things, to get our hands in the dirt. We needed a small starting place: a project that wasn't about what we could do but what we could watch. So my husband built a custom cedar planter for our patio.

Then one Saturday we loaded up our four children into the minivan and headed to the nursery. While my children wanted berry bushes and fruit trees, we settled on things that would fit in our raised bed planter: a few starter vegetables and herbs, tomatoes, celery, cucumber, basil, dill, rosemary, cilantro, and mint. We put in rocks for drainage and fresh soil. We lined up our few small plants and made holes with our shovels. We patted down the earth. My daughter eagerly hoisted the green plastic watering can and watered each plant diligently. We told our children that growing things takes time. We'd learn to care for the plants together; we'd practice patience.

Within days, the cucumber vines spilled over the edge and we noticed the popping yellow flowers. A few more days and little cucumbers dotted along the edges of vines. Each morning my daughter would head to the planter, water the vegetables, and run up the stairs excitedly showing me with her fingers how much her cucumber had grown. Some mornings when we discovered the leaves turning colors or a hole in a big green leaf, her joy would be stifled for a minute but then the refrain: "But Mama, we have more cucumbers, still!" We watched and waited, and something grew from nothing. Cucumbers were a miracle and waiting for them was magical.

• • •

But as we grow older, waiting feels like an inconvenience or affront. We take out our phones when we're waiting in the grocery store aisle for two minutes. We listen to podcasts on our commute. We leaf through magazines at the doctor's office. Waiting leaves us with a silence we don't know what to do with.

Impatience with waiting is nothing new. Like the antsy Israelites who built a golden calf because they were tired of waiting for Moses to come down from the mountain, we don't wait well.

Waiting evidences our limited autonomy and knowledge. We are subject to time and to conditions beyond our control. The seasons remind us of this: we plant seeds in the ground, but we cannot make things grow. Some plants, like the cucumber plant in our planter box, quickly sprout and spread; others never really get going. Like plants, we are subject to the loving care of our Father and the conditions in which he's placed us. And as much as we plan and make wise choices, we cannot control our lives.

Waiting reminds us that although we have agency, we are not ultimately in control. For those of us who find value in achieving, working hard, and crossing off tasks on our to-do lists, waiting can push us into a tailspin as it unhooks the lynchpin between who we are and what we do.

When forced to wait, we must reckon with the deep questions of identity. Who am I when I am not productive?

What if waiting weren't something to get past and hurdle over—a blip on our race to the top? What if waiting is an invitation to see ourselves as children again, dependent on a good Father?

When we learn to wait well, we get to leave behind the hustle that feels like anxiety, the sense we're always behind where we should be. When we wait well, we leave behind hurry; we slow down to see the beauty of being a creature, a part of God's good created order, not the masters who are responsible for keeping it all spinning. Waiting allows us to see ourselves as exuberant children, running to God to show him the state of the garden.

Waiting is good news: it is an invitation into a spacious life, not the barrier to it.

Waiting time isn't wasted time.

• • •

As for most things that matter, learning to wait well looks disorienting at first. When Jesus began his public ministry, he was first baptized in the Jordan River. The heavens peeled back like a page torn open, and the audible voice of God the Father told the waiting crowd that this was his beloved Son. Pleasure and affection surround the words of the Father. We imagine then that crowds will listen to him. Finally, he can leave his obscure, humble life and garner adulation, encouragement, and hit number one on all the charts.

But instead, after his baptism, Jesus is driven by the Spirit into a barren space, the wilderness, to fast and pray and to be tested by Satan. Matthew writes that the tempter came to Jesus, hissing in his ear the way he had done for Eve, pointing out his very real need for food. Hungry, tired, desirous of human companionship, Jesus heard the call of Satan for a quick fix to his physical problem.

Satan hits where it hurts: his belly and his identity. He says, "If you are the Son of God, command these stones to become loaves of bread" (Mt 4:3). He's asking Jesus to double down on his rights as the Son of God: If God had provided manna for his wayward people in the desert then surely the Son of God deserves the same provision (more so, even!). Shouldn't Jesus just show himself to be God's Son, race ahead of the Father's plan, throw out a few signs and wonders? Provide for his hunger pains? Didn't he deserve that?

We don't know the space of time between the temptation and Jesus' answer, or how much weight he'd lost from fasting, or the way identity can unravel piece by piece. We do know that Jesus was tempted like other people and he used the resources that we have, word and sacrament, to sustain him in the wilderness. He limited himself to the Father's plan—he chose to wait. Jesus waited well; he responded quoting Deuteronomy: "Man shall not live by bread alone, but by every word that comes from the mouth of God" (Mt 4:4). In other words: "Thanks, but no thanks, I'll wait on my dad."

Waiting well drives Jesus deeper into the good heart of his Father. Hurrying ahead or taking things before they are ready and ripe for the taking is the habit of the orphan. Waiting is trusting that our normal human limits aren't meant as defects but as guardrails that guide us to God.

> Waiting is trusting that our normal human limits aren't meant as defects but as guardrails that guide us to God.

How does Jesus wait well? Jesus isn't crafting grand metaphors about the Word of God being *like* food. There is a very real sense that though his body bore the effects of fasting, such as lacking nutrients and incurring weight loss, the Word of God nourishes the body of Christ, sustains the body of Christ, where the Word of God is, as F. Dale Bruner says, "so deep it can reach even the stomach." Perhaps it's because we're so prone to not waiting on God but instead attempting to control our circumstances that we can't fathom the Word of God actually nourishing us as food.

But what if we tried to practice waiting well—what would that look like?

• • •

With the global coronavirus pandemic in spring 2020, life stopped. Overwhelmed by the threat of a disease we couldn't stop and for which we didn't have the hospital capacity, everyone moved work and school into their homes. We were told our children would be back to school in three weeks. By then we'd flatten the curve and life would go back to normal. But as the months passed, as children didn't return to in-person classrooms in the fall, the waiting for "normal" to return seemed like riding a rollercoaster of depression, anxiety, fear, and listlessness. We could only wait.

There is a type of waiting where you remain walled off—you distract or numb yourself to move through time faster. You turn in on yourself. You fill up on salty chips, Netflix-bingeing, online political debate, or conjuring up imaginative vacation plans—anything to take you away from your own lack of control, your own unknowing.

There is another type of waiting where you lean into the pain to more deeply experience a peace that passes understanding. This is the sort of waiting we see Jesus do—leaning into his identity as a beloved son, feeding on the Word of God so that it nourishes his very body. This is the deep work of waiting, and while it feels barren, it strips us of our comforts so we can see what we're actually feeding on.

It's a gift to feel our hunger pains and, as children, to expect God will feed us.

As the pandemic wore on, I sat on my couch with the creeping realization that there were no good choices for schooling my four children in the upcoming school year. The small losses were like stones I stuck in my pockets. The weight would feel heavier with the drop of yet another one. I would not have long days of quiet to work, write, and go for long walks. Whether my children began their year distance learning with computers at home or we chose to homeschool them, we'd all be learning how to work, learn, and support one another together. We would be forced to wait: for "normal"; for a return to school, church, and activities; for a time when it felt safe enough to plan and dream again.

What if the cumulative weight of those rocks didn't drag me down but were like smooth stones I could turn over in my hands and offer as tangible prayers? What if all the anxieties that came flooding to the surface when I'm forced to wait could be cast out onto the water, skipping like smooth stones across a lake in the sure hand of the Father? What if I was being invited to wait not because God was displeased but *because he was pleased?*

I could also turn each new limit on my illusions of autonomy into a prayer. Each limit a chance to press into the nourishing Word. *Here, Father, take my fear about what comes next. Here, will you hold this wait of unknowing—it keeps me up at night? Could you show me, Father, how I could find joy even when it feels like I'm being closed in?*

What if all the limits on my ability to control, plan, and even dream, could be something that drew me deeper into the heart of God the Father? There is much good as we move through waiting with Jesus. But to wait well, we must first name the shape of our pain.

• • •

To stay soft to the Word of God, supple enough to feed on it as Jesus does in the wilderness, we must have the courage to draw contours around "the shape of our pain," as Seth Haines says. Being a human hurts. Acknowledging our own limits makes us feel weak.

In these dry and desert-like spaces, we may find the spacious place looks nothing like we thought. We're in a small closet and the lights don't work. This is not what we thought faith would be. But the path to a more spacious life—one of real freedom in Jesus where status, personality, performance, and what we have or don't have don't define us—always seems to lead us through the desert.

The pattern of a more spacious life often follows the pattern of Jesus' own life.

Walter Brueggemann writes that the movement of the psalms is from orientation to disorientation and then to new orientation. The psalms give us a language for transformation in desert spaces: we move from a particular view of ourselves, God, and the cosmos until suddenly we are disoriented by a sudden illness, pregnancy loss, a busted-up economy, being passed over for a job, news of global inequality, racial violence, and even the numbness of our own souls. As we wait, we are then invited to move through the limits that surface, to name the shape of our pain beneath, so that we can journey to reorientation.

What is the shape of your pain? Is your pain a gaping wound? Is it stuffed into the back corner of a closet, or is it neatly categorized and filed away with annotations that no one but you understand? Is your pain the hulking shadow, or does it come out in your careful planning and stockpiling?

Could you practice naming your pain's shape so God can heal you with words of life? When you do, do you see how God tenderly meets you in the pains you try to push down? Lean in: God invites us to name the shape of our pain so he can heal us with words of life. And when we do, he tenderly meets us.

• • •

In the early morning hours my husband and I sat together in the soft amber glow of a closet-turned-office, and we joined hands to pray. Tears dripped down my pajama shirt. Much of life felt like it was up for grabs—jobs unsure, future uncertain, choices narrowed, financial security confusing—and yet in the warm glow of light there was a steadiness that felt new, something warm and welcoming like the honeyed light.

Here we were again, our hands and lives open. We'd seen God provide thousands of dollars at the last minute. We'd seen him walk us through dark valleys of fear, betrayal, and the own dark parts we've played. We'd seen how he healed relational wounds.

So, as we sat in that small space that morning, feeling like we were hurtling to the edge of a cliff, uncertain of what would meet us on the other side, we told God who he had said he was because sometimes we fear he's forgotten. We repeated the nourishing word back to the eternal Word: *Fear not, I'm with you* (Is 41:10). *I will never leave you nor forsake you* (Heb 13:5). *I lavish steadfast love to a thousand generations* (Ex 20:6). *I am faithful and true* (Rev 19:11). *Remain in me* (Jn 15:4). This is who you are, God. Show yourself to be true.

In the amber light with our fingers intertwined, I speak words of the kindness of God, even when I don't see it. Dane Ortlund describes the bubbling, overflowing nature of Christ's heart toward us: "That God is rich in mercy means that your regions of deepest shame and regret are not hotels through which divine mercy passes but homes in which divine mercy abides. It means the things about you that make you cringe most, make him hug hardest." I said the words until I practiced believing them.

He is a kind parent who sees his children feeling alone and scared and wraps us in his strong and sturdy arms. When we tell him that the waiting hurts, and that we do not know how long we can hold on, we are not barred from communion with God but welcomed further up and further in.

All the limits that waiting brings up—fear of failure and the future, fear that our work is not good enough or we're not good enough, fear that we can't get a handle on sin or temptation or that we're never satisfied—are not places where God's nose is turned up in snobbish contempt but precisely the places where the heart of Jesus is drawn.

We are free to let the tears fall. To name back—sometimes in desperate, choking sobs—who God says he is. This is part of the hard work of waiting well.

Waiting well can also look like lament. I could stomp and rail at God (and I have), bringing my lament, pain, depression, and confusion to him. I lament with and for my brothers and sisters of color, as yet another brown or black man is killed. Waiting well looks like cries for justice. The people of God have cried, "How long, O Lord?" for centuries.

> Waiting well looks like cries for justice.

We continue to echo these words as we await the coming consummation of Jesus' kingdom. Lament and cries for justice are ways we wait well—as we remind God of his covenant promises and as we trust him to act and as we do works of mercy and justice in our communities.

This is how a spacious place grows within so that only Jesus can fill it. We ask him to prove himself faithful and true. We clench our jaw and stand on his steadfast love that extends to a thousand generations. We have a God who goes down with us through disorientation. We have a God who went to the desert places too.

It is not the waiting that is the thing, but rather, waiting opens us up so God can make his home in us. In the waiting, we are becoming. We'll find in those small spaces of our own soul the amber light shining through a crack, even in the places of deep pain and darkness.

> Waiting opens us up so God can make his home in us.

We think we can only find spaciousness when our circumstances are increasingly good. While you feel dizzy and confused waiting or in pain, hold on. Take heart, a spacious life cannot be found apart from wilderness moments. We must go *through* them—not numb them, run from them, stuff them down, or freeze them.

Our limits create for us a house in which God can dwell. Our limits create the texture of our conversation with God in waiting times. When we live the unlimited life full of hurry, we bypass eternal nourishment that can satisfy our deep hungers.

And our job as we wait isn't grand aerobatics but simply to hold on—or rather, to be held securely. When he sees us curled into the cleft of our sure foundation, perhaps the look on our Father's face is the same giddy delight on my daughter's when she's noticed a new cucumber: "Look!" she cries. "Come and see what's here! Isn't it amazing?"

• • •

Holy Spirit, the One who walked with Christ into the wilderness, would you gently show me the shape of my pain as I pause in silence now? When I'm lost in the disorientation of the wilderness, I confess the ways I've used you—Father, Son, and Spirit—as cheap answers, or spiritual genies.

God, you are faithful and true. You are enough. I long for a life where circumstances do not dictate my peace. Jesus, I claim your righteous triumph over my own temptation to hurry ahead and hustle my way out from this middle space of waiting. May your faithfulness restore my feeble spirit. Be with me, Lord Christ.

5

THE SPIRITUAL LIFE IS
NOT AN INSTANT POT

An Invitation to Rest

*f*ind a recipe from a famous cook. Throw in your frozen
chicken, baby red potatoes, ranch seasoning, and broth.
Push a button. And dinner arrives as quickly as Rosie made
it on *The Jetsons*. It's like magic. You don't have to wait for your
eggs to boil or your bone broth to cook down for two days. You
can enjoy chili from dried beans in hours or a pork shoulder
made effortlessly tender. The Instant Pot has swept the
nation—it is the world's first "viral cooking appliance." The
Instant Pot has saved time, made healthy meals accessible to
more people, and created tens of thousands of devotees to a
pressure cooker.

Yet I wonder if the Instant Pot (or any time-saving device) not only short-circuits our sense of time but also helps us re-imagine how transformation happens. When I cut my cooking time in half with a new gadget, I become accustomed to this new level of ease and dismiss the work and length of time that normally cooking would take. Every labor-saving and time-saving device shapes us. The questions we need to ask aren't simply about ease and convenience but about formation.

If I expect one tool to do so much, what am I gaining and what am I losing? And if we begin to feel that all of life should move at the speed of our devices, what do we do when we find our own spiritual lives terribly slow? We want to change our personal habits but find how deep the roots go and how vines of sin twist their way into our desires, habits, and actions. We become frustrated, expecting change to happen quickly.

• • •

The spiritual life is not an Instant Pot. It is in fact, as my spiritual director says, the slowest form of personal transformation. But how are we transformed? What connects the things we know about God to actually knowing God? How do we access a spacious life when our emotions are in shambles, or we've lost a child, or our neighbors are hurting?

We follow in the ancient paths—the daily and weekly habits that keep the household of faith running and thriving. These mundane acts of spiritual housekeeping—things like prayer, corporate worship, church community, Scripture reading, and care for our neighbor—connect us to God and each other, creating thick communities. The movement of spiritual transformation is slow, imperceptible at times, and yet when crisis hits, we will find we have a home in which to shelter. We've done the laundry of our souls, so to speak, so we have some clean socks to wear. The invitation to rest is where we begin.

• • •

When I lived in an affluent suburb, the unlimited life looked like women fueled by coffee, workouts, and winding down with wine. We spent our afternoons driving children to practices and math groups. To earn love, we stayed small, put healthy-ish meals on the table, and got the kids where they needed to go. And in our haste we wondered where we'd gone. Feeling out of touch with the meatier things of life, many of us opted for spa days, Target runs, and book clubs that we hoped would bring levity, camaraderie, and hope.

Men felt disconnected from the lives of their children, working long hours to afford "the good life." But when they were home, they were all there—they were in classrooms and coaching on basketball courts and walking children to school. They worked to provide the vacations as a reward for all the work they had done: as if a week in Hawaii or skiing in Colorado would replenish our weary and worn-out souls.

Everyone was "all in"—for the good of our children; for our jobs, our hobbies, our political causes; for our arts or ministry. But the "all in" life always asked more of us—more time, energy, emotion—and it left us empty and exhausted.

A life without limits is a life of constant hurry and comparison, and underneath it all, a sense that we must always keep earning our worth. We're stuck in an Instant Pot life: we hope that working harder, achieving more, and doing more will be the ingredients that will create the feast of a good life. All in record time.

In pursuit of freedom, we instead serve our work. We are desperate for rest and so very fearful of it.

• • •

One recent Sunday, I woke up slowly, without an alarm. My husband wasn't preaching that week, and so instead of looking over his sermon in the wee hours of the morning, he kindly remembered how wonderful it feels for me to be served a hot cup of coffee in bed

> We are desperate for rest and so very fearful of it.

in my favorite mug. Blue earthenware mug in hand, I sat looking out my bedroom window, the sky glowing a faint pink. The house was quiet and the day slowly unfurled. I sat in bed a bit longer, thanking God.

We went to worship. I taught Sunday school with my middle schooler as my teaching assistant, remembering how God promised through Obadiah that he would save his covenant people. We enjoyed blueberry lemonade and Mediterranean food with the guest preacher and his wife. At home phones stayed plugged in on the counters and social media was deleted for the day. We took naps. We made love. We enjoyed our children and ate dessert first—our Sabbath practice so our children will remember how sweet the Lord's day is, as Jewish children have been awoken with honey on their tongues.

We put the pot roast in to cook all afternoon and enjoyed rich wine with our meat, roasted vegetables, and crusty bread. As a family, we played a game and watched a show together. I took a bath and then brought a book to bed, where we prayed for "a peaceful night and a perfect end." In short, the rest of God was both luxurious and simple.

Sabbath begins in rest. The Jewish people practice Shabbat sundown on Friday to sundown on Saturday. It begins and ends in the dark, where rest (not hustle) is the first word. "Hurry does violence to the soul," but rest restores us. And rest is not simply a pause that restores us; it actually re-stories us, putting us back into the story of God with all our human limits. We can form habits that create the conditions for rest, but rest is ultimately a gift given by a good God.

> We can form habits that create the conditions for rest, but rest is ultimately a gift given by a good God.

Sabbath is a day for reorienting our bodies, minds, and souls into our proper place—rejoicing in our creatureliness. We need rest, good food and drink, and a slower pace to worship our Maker. This is the work we were made to do, for all of life—from the mundane to the monumental—is to be given back in worship, to accept the grace of rest as good, and to walk in step with the Spirit of God.

• • •

When Jesus began his ministry after the wilderness temptations, he called to himself disciples. They left their nets in the water when he told them they'd be fishers of men. Early on in their discipleship, they watched Jesus teach about the kingdom of God. They saw how he welcomed outcasts, lepers, Gentiles, and women into his ministry.

And then they learned about his lordship in a boat.

Jesus settled in for a nap. While out on the Sea of Galilee, there was a storm, and the boat was suddenly swamped by waves, water crashing in on all sides. They bailed as much out as they could, but their knees were wet. Though experienced fishermen, they had never been in a storm like this. The waves kept coming. The wind was whipping around them and they felt done in. How was Jesus still sleeping? Overwhelmed with anxieties, they woke him up with staccato shouts: "Lord! Save! Dying!"

The man Jesus got up groggily, and as waves crashed in, he looked them in the eyes: "Why are you such cowards? Littlefaiths!"

He turned his attention to the mountain of water: "Be still." The sea became like glass. The disciples' beating hearts began to slow. "Who is this?" they wondered. He is the one who, as the psalmist says, "stills the roaring of the seas, the roaring of their waves" (Ps 65:7). He is the Lord of earth and sea. Yet he is also one who naps: "The Lord in heaven neither sleeps nor slumbers, but on earth, as true man, he does."

Jesus showed himself as Emmanuel, God with us: his divine power revealed in power over creation itself and his full humanity shown in his need for a nap.

• • •

The invitation to rest is two-pronged: it is an invitation to heed the limits of our bodies (to slow down, rest, and sleep) and to reorient ourselves toward God as dependent children instead of productive machines (ceasing from work, practicing sabbath).

When we choose sleep, we rest in our limitations as created beings. When we sleep, we admit our limits: we are needy creatures. We exist within the bookends of God's own creation and care. Our joyful response is to sleep. The order of the universe is always grace first: we receive first and then we work in response to the rest and care we've been given. We do not work for rest or in order to earn our rest. We start with rest.

We accept that we are incapable of doing for ourselves what sleep provides. Through sleep our brains, muscles, and hormones function better; our cells are repaired; our energy is conserved. But sleep is not simply useful in the increased health and productivity it provides—a means to further self-centered work. Sleep is a gift.

Sleep is a sort of mini-sabbath where we accept our bodily limits and embrace our humanity. Sleeping replenishes more than our physical bodies: sleep "is a declaration of trust. It is admitting that we are not God (who never sleeps), and that is good news."

• • •

What allows Jesus to sleep in the midst of chaos? The only times we hear the audible voice of God the Father in the New Testament he is saying the same thing about Jesus: *This is my boy. He is loved. I'm so proud of him. Listen to him.* As Jesus comes up from the waters of baptism, before he had healed, or taught, or done anything remarkable, Jesus received the blessing of his Father simply for being his. His identity as *son* informs his work and worship. It is from that union with the Father that the whole life of Christ turns. Healing, wisdom, cutting words of truth, and the kind touch of compassion all flow from Jesus' union with the Father. This is what informs his sleep.

Jesus sleeps because he needs to, *and* he sleeps because he has nothing to prove.

How about you? Sleep may be the first spiritual discipline we can do to practically place ourselves in a position of being a son or daughter of God. It is those who eat the "bread of anxious toil" who neglect sleep, who need to keep working to be worthy (Ps 127:2).

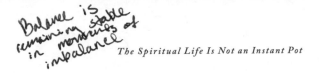

But how do overwork and hustle bar us from rest? It's easy to chastise the guy in the corner office or on a political drama for working too much, but what about us? Do we schedule too many meetings, church small groups, kids' activities, mercy ministry opportunities, so that we've made ourselves indispensable to God's work in the world? Rest isn't just about sleep, even when we've pushed ourselves past our limits. Rest is also about choosing to cease from overwork, and on one day a week to rest from our labors, placing ourselves into the sustaining hands of our Maker.

Rest is the bodily antidote to hurry and hustle.

We are given agency, stewardship, and the blessing of partnering with God in the work he's already doing, but when our workaholism turns these good things into identity markers, we are not heeding God's invitation to rest. Resting from our work at appropriate times in the day and in a weekly Sabbath shifts

> Rest is the bodily antidote to hurry and hustle.

the balance. We are recipients of God's care, not the sole purveyors of it.

Our workaholism and distraction show our little faith. Yet Jesus does not shame his disciples for being "littlefaiths." He comes to their aid, and ours, whether our faith is great or small.

It is not the strength of our faith that gets Jesus to act. He acts according to his own nature: he brings order from chaos; he is Lord of all. We are invited to cover ourselves with his power, name our own limitations, and find rest in them.

• • •

We want a firework spirituality: explosive, colorful, dynamic, eliciting oohs and ahs. Practices like sleep and sabbath seem too mundane to make a difference. They're like household chores we ignore or outsource, like the monotonous tasks of laundry, dishwashing, and vacuuming. Yet spiritual disciplines are the household chores of God's family. They are how we get the Christian life in us.

In Psalm 65, after describing God's power over the seas, the psalmist writes:

> You crown the year with your bounty;
>   your wagon tracks overflow with abundance.
> The pastures of the wilderness overflow. (Ps 65:11-12)

Spiritual disciplines are like well-worn wagon tracks, the ancient paths that we follow because they've been cut out by a competent guide and found to be good and effective ways of traveling through terrain. Wagon tracks aren't sexy, but they do mark out the faithful way.

Prioritizing sleep is a habit that shapes us. So is choosing to abide by God-given limits of our time for our week. These habits remind us that we are not lords of time but are subject to it. And rather than making time be productive (where we divide it up into optimally efficient increments), we choose to inhabit time, like we inhabit a place. When we structure our time according to the well-worn paths that God has given to show us how we work best, we find time not hurrying by but a place to live and worship, like a house or cathedral. This sense of time, what Heschel called "an architecture of time," happens when we rest, when we practice sabbath, and when our work finds its proper place in our days.

When we live in time like a place, we find a sense of spaciousness: the slow morning, the chance to play, the cup of coffee in bed, the lingering over worship, or a fine line of poetry, or sex, or a good meal—these all become gifts that remind us who we are. When we sleep or when we practice sabbath, we are choosing to accept that we cannot *do* in order to be loved: identity is given and conferred by God alone.

When I teach my children how to clear their plates, or operate the washing machine, or cook salmon, I go step by step. We go slowly. I don't expect them to know adult ways of doing things yet. It would be ridiculous to shame them for not knowing or to present them with a long manual with too-big-sounding words as instructions. They are "littlefaiths." They need my hands helping, showing them the proper amount of laundry detergent, and they need gentle instructions to pay attention to the heat coming from the oven and stove. As we practice our faith—through something as small as sleep and something as life-changing as resting for twenty-four hours as a sabbath to the Lord—we grow from littlefaiths into a house where we all can find sustenance and shelter.

Sabbath and sleep allow us to enter our day with the same anticipation and awe as if we were entering a cathedral.

It is only as we practice the habits of faith that we will find ourselves not simply understanding facts about Jesus but known by him. It is only as we do the small, repeated household tasks of the family of God that we will be able to access the spacious life even when life's circumstances are cramped and unknown.

So take a nap. You are a child of the God who stills the wind and the waves from without and within.

• • •

Lord of heaven and earth, I confess I choose work over rest. I try to make my own way. My faith is little. I want spectacular and flashy. I want exciting experiences to buoy me, not the wagon tracks of faith. But as I choose these housekeeping habits—things like rest and sabbath—would you grow my little faith?

Only you Lord make me dwell in safety (Ps 4:8). Grant me a peaceful night and a perfect end.

Help me sleep knowing you watch over me as I do. Amen.

6

FLYING KITES ON THE EDGE OF THE SEA

An Invitation to Delight

*t*he light was gentle, like pink spun sugar; gold dropped into the ocean. The gulls soared and dove over the palm trees on the knife edge of dusk. They turned, falling into the wind. They floated and hovered. Bird-like, a kite, soared a mile high.

We had brought our picnic dinner to this bluff overlooking the sea. We unpacked the charcuterie and poured a glass of wine. We munched on nuts. There was room for our children to run and play. Seeing the kite, my kids were fascinated: How does it fly so high? How much string does that man have? How is it not tangled in trees? So, laughing and cartwheeling, they met Nico, the kite flyer, who was wearing Ray-Bans and Levi's.

As children so easily do, they asked questions, made conversation, and entered unselfconsciously into another's story.

He let them hold the line so they could feel the kite in the sky pull in the wind—as if air were thick and solid. Nico told us stories of his home in Afghanistan, where boys would run for kites. He told us how kite-flying crossed an ocean and a continent and then found a home in the Bay Area. There they would compete for kites. And like kites, there were in Nico and the others two cultures and two stories fighting and getting tangled. Nico invited me over, and I felt the taut line. He told us the delicate tissue was getting wet from the sea air a mile up.

Below us the ocean met the sand. Above us, the mama birds called their babies home as the light waned. Nico pulled in the line with gentle fingertips. As we said thank you and returned to our meal, I smiled. I had wanted to be alone, and yet here I had an invitation to marvel about pink skies and flying birds, right alongside my children.

• • •

The spacious place God has for us is something more than cycling between production and escape—where we overschedule and overwork, and then collapse in exhaustion. These are the rhythms of our achievement-oriented society. A spacious life is more than treating our minds, bodies, and hearts as if they were machines of repetitive doing to be plugged back in to charge for the next day.

The hurried life is a slow creep back into busy habits— habits that do more than take up our time; they also take up space in the soul for creativity, growth, and the slow work of transformation.

It begins like this: We resolve to eat family dinners five days a week, but Ezra wants to try out for club soccer so we drive a further twenty minutes two days a week after school. Porter's soccer schedule is (of course) on alternating days and Camden takes up golf with his grandparents. We accommodate the schedules of those in our church, so our community group can meet another night of the week. And then there is the weekly-or-so evening meeting that pops up on my husband's calendar. We say yes to too many events in our home without having a down week to recover.

On nights when we're home, we unthinkingly turn on the TV because we don't have the energy for conversation or a board game. The hurried life is ordering my day according to deadlines and others' expectations of me, instead of vulnerably giving myself to the moment at hand, the task at hand, and the person at hand. It happens bit by bit, without us even realizing this is the script we're following.

We think a hurried life will get us to a meaningful life, but while our schedules are packed, we have precious little depth to show for it. Hurry always lets us down.

Freedom isn't stuffing more on your calendar to feel good enough. We'll find freedom—not in the absence of constraints but in the presence of loving ones. A week to recover from a busy week. A slow night reading by the fire. Saying no to the PTA meeting, sports schedule, or last-minute request to volunteer.

> We'll find freedom—not in the absence of constraints but in the presence of loving ones.

Our noes make room for the right yeses.

And when we have a bit more room, we find ourselves welcomed into delight, something we forfeit through hurry. Delight is like my children making forts with neighborhood kids in a nearby tree. They would spend hours with a few rudimentary tools and weave branches in their joint construction project. A saw, twine, and some fallen branches provided all they needed to create a place of creativity and imagination—a place that was theirs, away from the world of adult responsibilities. Delighted with their work, creativity actually flourishes within limits.

Though we think our limits put a lid on wonder, they actually invite wonder to go deeper. A spacious life holds out delight not as a reward for hard work but as an invitation. Our delight is a response to God's delight in us.

You are delighted in. You are held securely in the firm and steady grip of a good and kind Father. You are welcomed into the practice of delight because God delights in you.

• • •

Maybe you think of Jesus as slightly melancholy, our somber Savior, a "man of sorrows" wandering the Judean hillsides, often struck with compassion for the crowds and healing diseases. While he did experience sorrow and compassion, what about laughter, joy, and delight?

Jesus reclined at table. The guest list was thick with thieves and other "sinners." The religious folks considered him a drunkard by the company he kept. It's unlikely that he kept to himself at these dinners, a wallflower worried about what people would say. Their imperfection could not tarnish the perfection of Christ.

So he ate and drank heartily. I imagine him laughing, perhaps getting a bit teary-eyed as his in-the-flesh dinners were shadows of the coming marriage supper of the Lamb.

He enjoyed these people. The rabble-rousers, the drunks, the liars and cheats, the demon-possessed and prostitutes, all found a welcome with Jesus. Jesus invited himself over to the home of Zacchaeus, a reviled tax collector. He said, "I must stay at your house today" (Lk 19:5). The poor, needy, and reviled found a welcome so rich and deep it changed them.

Little children knew him to be safe and good. They wanted to be with him. Jesus beckoned them to come to him, against the protests of his disciples. It's unlikely Jesus lectured the children on fine theological points. I imagine him as the fun uncle with the neighborhood kids, doing what uncles do best: play.

This undercurrent of delight often goes unmentioned in the Gospels, perhaps because it's assumed. So far away culturally from first-century Jewish life, we cannot see the joy implicit in the timekeeping of the Jewish people. Jesus grew up with weekly Sabbaths and yearly festivals (timed with the new moon for more light for more celebration) so that the people of God could gather, feast, and place themselves in the wider story of God's redemption. These festivals, as the apostle Paul says, are "a shadow of the things to come," harbingers of the great marriage supper of the Lamb when Jesus is reunited to his people in glory (Col 2:17). B. B. Warfield remarks, "If our Lord was 'the Man of Sorrows,' he was more profoundly still, 'the Man of Joy.'" While we might hear little of this delight overtly stated in the Gospels, it is a thread woven throughout Jesus' life.

All the feasts and festivals point to this final joy, where our joy is complete, satiated by the presence of God. Our God is a God of joyful delight. The three persons of the Trinity indwell one another. As Augustine put it, the Godhead, "the supreme source of all things, and the most perfect beauty, and the most perfect delight," is related mysteriously together: "Each are in each, and all in each, and each in all, and all are." While we mightn't be able to mentally grasp the three-in-oneness of God, it's worth paying attention to a common metaphor the early church fathers used to describe the Trinity: a dance. A dance can be participatory, revelatory, intimate, and full of delight.

Jesus didn't need to look for delight, just as we might find ourselves unexpectedly delighted by a surprise gift or a beautiful sunset. Jesus, from time eternal has been in a dance of joy, mutual self-giving, and love with God the Father and God the Spirit. He then, as it were, moves his dance steps down to earth. Jesus prays that his followers "may have my joy fulfilled in themselves" (Jn 17:13). It multiplies. His delight begets more delight.

When he called his disciples to follow him, when he invited the children to come to him, when he sat down and ate good food, these were all ways he extended the invitation to delight in the perfect love of God.

• • •

Delight is an appropriate response to being loved by God. The psalmist tells us it is God's delight that motivates his care: "He brought me out into a spacious place; he rescued me because he delighted in me" (Ps 18:19 NIV). God's delight prompts his provision, his rescue. The spacious place isn't the result of earning it or hurrying to achieve it. God delights in us because we are his. He reaches down, picks us up, and brings us out into a spacious place. He offers in himself a hiding place, a cleft in the rock, a horn of salvation, and a stronghold (Ps 18:2). As God delights in us, he teaches us how to delight in him.

To be full, delight always needs another. It is in the loving eyes of my husband that I see myself rightly, not in words of comparison or self-condemnation. Delight woos us back to our deepest identity: we are children loved and redeemed by God. And what tends to emerge from delight? Play. Have you noticed it is confident children—not stoic, put-together, hurried, and harried adults—who play?

Play is our response to the deep-in-our-bones sense that God delights in us.

As Brazilian theologian Rubem Azevedo Alves tells us, our world is controlled by production and consumption, and play subverts this story. Delight restores to us some of the nonconsumable parts of our humanity: how we run fabric through our fingers, or enjoy the clink of glasses, the feel of a particular blanket, the laughter of a child, the textures in a bouquet, or the well thought-out sentence in a newspaper column. Or the arcs in the air made by birds or kites.

Last summer the temperatures had become so high that every word I spoke sounded cranky, because I was. So I told my four kids to grab their swimsuits and we walked to the neighborhood pool. Instead of reading by the side of the water, I jumped in, eager for cool water to calm my nerves and cool my skin. While they splashed and played, I tucked my feet up

> Play is our response to the deep-in-our-bones sense that God delights in us.

on the bumpy wall of the pool and did back dives, feeling the water across my arched back and middle. The water went up my nose—that waterlogged feeling came rushing back of childhood summer days in the pool playing sharks and minnows until my eyes were bloodshot and I would use my spare change to buy a candy bar and Cactus Cooler soda. I held my breath and did a handstand like I was a girl. I played my children's games of chase across the pool. We had nothing to accomplish but laughter.

There was a lightness born of floating in cool chlorinated water and a deeper lightness from engaging in the rhythms of childhood. It wasn't the cycle of production and escape, where I work too hard and then escape to Netflix or to my closet to stealthily eat chocolate. Play breaks the cycle. It reestablishes our feet on a path that leads to green pastures—or, at least, pool water.

• • •

Can we delight in God the way he delights in us? When I abandon the hurried life long enough to slow down and play with my children, the fabric of our relationship is strengthened.

Risk is a primary part of play. As a child you may have spent hours learning a skill—riding a bike or getting up the nerve to do the monkey bars. As a child begins, she reaches out and tries to grab the first rung. She may fall, but she keeps trying. As adults, we don't tell her she's failing at the monkey bars. Instead, we know she's learning and practicing. The child instinctively knows it'll be fun to swing, so the practice and the returning to the task are all in the service to the future end: delight. Swinging may feel like flying, and she can't wait to get there.

So I practice the risky first moves of delighting in God just like learning the monkey bars. I settle into this question: Can I play with God? Can I turn off the drive to do and practice being with him—even if it feels awkward and I'm unsure if I'll be able to hear him?

I sit in silence, breathing in and out. I think of Jesus calling his first disciples—how something magnetic pulled at each man as he left his fishing nets or tax collector's booth. I imagine him walking along the edge of the water, tossing out the simple words like a net: "Follow me."

They don't know what will happen when they drop their lives into the hands of this man Jesus. Perhaps it feels a bit like flying or jumping into risk. Will they be caught and held as they jump? If not, will they dust themselves off laughing, and try again?

I borrow words from Scripture and well-worn prayers. I rehearse centuries-old words: "Preserve us from faithless fears and worldly anxieties, and grant that no clouds of this mortal life may hide from us the light of that love which is immortal." I try drawing my prayers. I go for walks and smile at the sunshine and think about sharing a smile with God at the world he's created. I think of that moment when I'm underwater and how maybe being "preserved from external worry" feels like that quiet space. If we eschew hurry, we might wear the immortal love of God. But we have to risk, to throw our bodies toward the next monkey bar.

As I practice these alternate habits to hurry—the being instead of doing, the praying instead of fretting—the muscles of faith strengthen. So when we suddenly found our lives upside down after that evening on the bluffs and then had to navigate change and transition, I told friends when they asked: "Yes, we're okay. We don't know what's next. It feels a bit like free fall." But there is something else there too: a buoyancy that nevertheless feels secure, as we dot-to-dot God's faithfulness through decades.

He has never let us go. He has always been with us. We have always had food and a roof over our heads, and though I know this is never promised to us, he has proven himself to be Emmanuel, the God who cares and the God who laughs.

• • •

Play, no matter its form, grows in safety and flourishes because of limitations. From our point of view, our own risk feels deadly serious and frightening, but I imagine God looking on from the playground bench, smiling at how we keep at it. He knows we are seen and ultimately safe. We are in midair between the letting go and the holding on. And while we've let go, we remember that we are also held. We have a place to come home to in the prayers, in the reading of Scripture, in Communion, and as we gather together. We are free to play because we belong.

Do you play still?

Our play doesn't need to be good; it just comes from a secure identity in God, our Father who sees us. It comes from our willingness to be like little chicks peeping and gathered under the wings of Jesus (Lk 13:34). It's okay if we're a little rusty. I have a hard time knowing what playing dolls with my six-year-old should look like, so I more often shoo her outside to play with her brothers instead. Play calls attention to our weak muscles of delight. But we can keep trying.

After all, play is an act of protest against value and worth being measured by what we produce. It reminds us that human dignity is conferred because creation itself is God's act of play. Only the unlimited One could create a cosmos full of galaxies known only to him, populate the depths of the sea with fishes with flashlights on their heads, create cheetahs and sloths, ecosystems and laws of nature.

> Play is an act of protest against value and worth being measured by what we produce.

And what about us, the limited ones? To play is to participate in the habits that shape our identity toward trusting our unlimited God with our limited lives. It is good that we are limited. When we embrace our tiredness, our fear of risk taking, our inability to make good soup or play dolls with our children, we remember we are not productive machines. We are people, and better than that, we are loved children held in the sure grip of a good Father who lets us dive and soar and never lets us go.

So play with sentences, dance in your kitchen, learn something new, engage someone in conversation—stake your claim in a million small ways that you are held even as you leap.

What if play were your revolutionary way of asserting this bold claim: I am more than what I produce, what or who I know, or what ladder I climb? You could be free to be silly or make a fool of yourself.

What if you could stop measuring yourself by your to-do list and find yourself, like Nico's kite, diving and playing in a wide-open space and yet anchored too in the hands of a kind Father—what then? It might feel like freedom, like a dance of delight, like doing exactly what you're meant to do. You have a long line connecting you to safety. You can play. You have nothing to prove.

• • •

Lord Christ, you had a small life delighting in the affection of your Father, content to walk in the paths of the living God. Yet too from eternity past delight was the dance of the Trinity. May I hide myself so deeply in your own affections that I have the courage to bring my whole self to you. Help me to play and help me bring others in. Thank you for holding me tightly. Amen.

7

LOVE ISN'T A COCKTAIL PARTY

An Invitation to Pay Attention

i have a bad habit I hope I'm learning to break: I walk into a room and tell everyone about the latest thing I've read or thought about, which would be fine if I were at a cocktail party wearing pearls and heels. But my life is not a cocktail party.

I may fancy myself interesting, pulling out thoughtful topics and threading them together, but often this looks less like witty banter with canapés and more like a bulldozer. My family is in the midst of doing other things—reading, watching sports, or doing chores—and when I waltz in with my knowledge du jour, I am simply not paying attention. Their own attention is broken. In my desire to tell everyone what I know or to accomplish a task I want done, it's easy to bypass the actual people in front of me.

I have failed to notice, to pay attention to others in the same manner I've paid attention to myself.

While we tend to excuse these as "quirks of character" in ourselves (and perhaps in others), when we do so, we fail to see all of life under the two plumb lines of Jesus: loving God and loving neighbor. How can we love our neighbor when we do not listen to them?

While some groups get gratification from speaking over one another (creating a sort of tapestry of ideas and loud opinions), this is not the way of the people I live with. So part of loving my neighbor means paying attention to specific people, not people in general. Growth in grace for me now means constraint, not self-expression, or rather, self-expression within the confines of love. I am learning that love too is a discipline. Love flourishes best within boundaries.

It's not that I'm not paying attention at all: I love paying attention to the things I want to pay attention to. But attention, like freedom, must be given away. If attention is a form of prayer, like Simone Weil said, then I tend to live a life of anti-prayer. I wonder what might happen in the fabric of our collective lives if I practiced stopping, listening first, seeing, and paying attention.

• • •

Jesus' ministry was a ministry of paying attention.

One time, Jesus is teaching in the temple and suddenly stops. Everyone turns to look. He sees a woman whose body is bent in two. Jesus not only notices her but stops his holy work to turn his attention toward her. This too is holy work. He calls her to him. He frees her from this disabling spirit and she stands up straight, praising God.

Another time, Jesus sees the fear in Nicodemus, coming, as he does, to Jesus in the middle of the night. Jesus answers questions Nicodemus is too afraid to ask, telling him salvation comes through the winds of the Spirit. He must be born again.

He also sees an unclean Samaritan woman as an image bearer—not simply as a type, as an ideological enemy to the Jews. Sentence by sentence, Jesus beautifully offers her living water instead of shame.

He sees children and women, the outcasts and forgotten. He feeds the poor. He heals the centurion's son and commends the father's faith, who holds rank and ethnic superiority over this prophet from Galilee. Everywhere Jesus goes, he sees people others overlook: the poor, the marginalized, and the widow. Healing often follows Jesus' compassionate attention, given especially to the ones society has forgotten.

He sees those in authority too. For the haughty, proud, and religious leaders—those trying to use power and position to transgress their common human limits—he has words of admonishment, or invitations to repentance, or parables to help them see the clouded state of their own hearts.

In Jesus' parable of the Good Samaritan, whereas the priest and the Levite only pay attention to the letter of the law and their holy to-do lists, it is the Samaritan who tends to the bleeding man on the side of the road. The practice of the Samaritan's attention-keeping brings life.

Jesus is interruptible. He has time for people.

Jesus' ministry was a ministry of attention because he first paid attention to the voice of his Father through Scripture and prayer. He knew the Father's beating heart, and he knew how to hide himself there so that he could then see others.

As we read through the Gospels, we mustn't forget that the majority of Jesus' life was a quiet one. Born to poor parents,

Jesus is interruptible. He has time for people.

following in the family business, reading and meditating on the Torah, and praying were the substance of his days. He was subject to family demands and household tasks.

The years before his public ministry deeply formed him too. We see Jesus' focus on cultivating quiet: how he often leaves for desolate places to pray even during his itinerant teaching and healing. We know he had a love for God his Father and an understanding of his Word so that at age twelve, he amazed the teachers of the law with his wisdom and authority.

Today will we stop hurrying long enough to pay attention to our own soul and to the quiet voice of God?

• • •

When we have twenty-five browser tabs open at all times, no margin in our calendars, and ten-year plans, and find ourselves trying to listen to podcasts, kick the dishwasher closed, make dinner, and help children with homework all at the same time, it's no wonder attention eludes us.

Our modern Western world holds out a fast-paced life as a ticket to freedom. If we hurry now, we can rest later. We look forward to a more spacious place one day in the future: once the promotion comes, or the vacation, or the kids leave home. But we're unable to access a "peace that passes understanding" in the tumult of daily life. Our fuses are short with others, we have an inner agitation we can't shake, our cortisol levels increase, and we find ourselves out of place. We are hurrying through our lives. But as John Mark Comer reminds us, "Hurry and love are incompatible." If paying attention to another is what love looks like, then hurry betrays our love is more often curved in on itself.

We cannot seem to even cross off the tasks on our to-do lists, let alone accomplish what we desire. Yet the art of paying attention acknowledges our limited time and follows Jesus in spending it in the same way Jesus does: in love and prayer. When we practice paying attention, we embrace our limits of time.

• • •

In our restless and harried twenty-first century, attention is a radical form of love. How can you practice paying attention as an act of love? How might you embrace your own limits of time?

A good diagnostic question is: What happens when you try to be still? Do the doubts creep in, do you simply distract yourself with your phone? Do you feel "not enough" because you aren't "good enough"? Rather than stuffing or distracting, pay attention to the hurry in your soul. In the process, bring that attention back to Jesus.

Remember how he stilled the waves or dined at Simon the leper's home, how he called down Zacchaeus from the tree and told him he'd eat with him. Can you sit with God in the silence? Can you read the stories and ask God where you need the attention of Christ? Do you need him to call you down, or to touch the dying parts of yourself, or offer you living water instead of the spiritual soda you fill up on?

When we realize the extent to which we are the broken man on the side of the road, the bleeding woman, the man who can't see, or the woman laid low with shame, we begin to ask the curious questions of attention:

What is my true estate?

What do I need?

What in me needs healing or needs to be seen?

Jesus looks at us with wide and kind attention. From this gaze of love, he bandages up our soul's wounds and brings us out into a spacious place. Under such a perfect loving gaze, the Spirit allows us to pay attention to all the ways we are loved and yet also fall short: he draws us into repentance. We may pay attention to the ways we do not respect our temporal limits, how we stuff things in our souls, how we hurry past God and others.

We have a great disconnect between the life of the follower of Jesus in the Bible and our own hurried ones. We go to church and we may read our Bibles occasionally, but we're not experiencing the easy yoke Jesus promises. Why? Dallas Willard tells us: "The general human failing is to want what is right and important, but at the same time not to commit to the kind of life that will produce action we know to be right and the condition we want to enjoy." Practicing paying attention—to the movements in our souls, to the Word of God, to those around us—becomes how we live the spacious life we want.

We must slow down and attend to this reality: we care more for what hurry can bring us than the slow way of Jesus. We do not want to commit ourselves to the patient seeing of others, to communing with God and asking what he requires, or to a gentle attention to ourselves when we are sad, angry, or confused. Hurry feels safer.

Let us have the courage to start in the dark closets of our souls and let Jesus heal what we are using hurry to mask. Maybe it's a fear of being used up and worthless, or being no longer young, beautiful, and vibrant. Maybe we've operated so long in a state of hurry that we've lost dreams and desires and we're afraid to be cracked open.

We need Jesus to touch us. We need the Spirit to awaken us. We notice our lack of attention, we repent of our hurry, we pray for the attentive awakening touch of Christ, and we pray to be drawn into a life of love: a life of attention to God and neighbor.

What will you do with your one, limited life? What will you do with your limited time? Will you dare to pay attention?

• • •

In John 12, Mary anoints Jesus' feet at Bethany with a pound of expensive perfume and burial incense. Mary enters the room with her hair down. All is silent, except for the sound of the jar cracked open. She begins to rub her hands on Jesus' feet. The perfume goes everywhere, dripping off of his feet and soaking into the ground. The room is filled with its smell. She rubs his feet with her hair. The men watch; their mouths open hinges.

This feels too lavish, something intimate made public. The guests move uncomfortably in their seats. Love exposes us. We judge. We keep our distance from that kind of love: Judas Iscariot asks incredulously, "Why wasn't this perfume sold and the money given to the poor?" (Jn 12:5 NIV).

But the attention Jesus had paid to Mary led to worship. It led to extravagant love. Through the course of Jesus' ministry, he saw her. He had raised her brother from the dead. She had sat at his feet. Now she pays attention to him, knows him as her Lord, and so, worshipfully anoints him as king and, perhaps doing more than she knows, prepares his body for burial.

When the king has paid attention to us, when the Spirit has opened our eyes, when we see ourselves rightly and our wounds in need of tending, we will be drawn further in to worship. It may be mundane like our daily Bible reading and prayer. Or it may look lavish and costly. Worship will then spill over so that the whole "house" of our lives will be "filled with the fragrance of the perfume" (Jn 12:3). Worship then moves us outward, to pay attention to others.

Even small acts of attention can bind up wounds and be the very fragrance of Christ. Last spring, a friend stopped by unexpectedly with a candle and pack of tea from Trader Joe's for me. Tears suddenly came to my eyes. While she had fretted a bit about candle scents, I felt seen. When I had disappointing news, another friend took a moment to pray my desires back to me. It had been a long time since I'd been seen in such small and deeply meaningful ways.

> Even small acts of attention can bind up wounds and be the very fragrance of Christ.

Paying attention is as small as a posture, a tone of voice, a moment of time. We bend down to speak to a child. We halt the exasperated tone in our voice about the chore left undone. We buy the grieving family dinner and gladly accept the casserole left on our porch when life is overwhelming. Small practices of seeing our neighbors strengthens our attention-keeping muscles so we begin to see the ones Jesus saw: those on the margins that our hurry and hustle move us past too quickly. We pay attention to the stories of children separated from parents in detention centers. We give the voiceless a voice by using our own resources to bring these stories to the attention of those in power.

If we are to be friends of Jesus, the ones more apt to use the jar of perfume than to condemn its use, we will practice paying attention to ourselves, to God, and to others.

Perhaps we do not hear the voice of God because we have stopped paying attention; we have instead filled up our time like filling up our homes with knickknacks or piles of papers we think we will need someday. We need a clear out like one we had for our home last year. In our day of purging, my husband wisely told me to not look in the trash can. He knew if I did, I'd likely gather back the odd memento I thought would make me happy, but instead I would soon find myself overrun by stuff. Wanting a more spacious home that bends around hospitality, beauty, and meaning, I kept the trashcan lid closed. I trusted his judgment because he wants good things for me and for us, and he knows my limits.

God knows you. His desire is not to rob you of things you need, but to wisely help make room in your attention for the things of his kingdom. So as the Spirit brings us into the dark and dingy corners of our souls where we realize the extent to which we've been chasing a freedom that has, in fact, caged us, may we see how the gospel is, as Malcolm Guite writes, "not only making the space but taking the time for the kingdom that might seem tiny as a mustard seed but will prove,

> His desire is not to rob you of things you need, but to wisely help make room in your attention for the things of his kingdom.

in due course, to be the great branching tree in whose canopy we all find a place. But we must glimpse the seed, buy the field, take the time, and not lose it all by 'hurrying by.'"

Make the space. Take the time. Glimpse the seed. Practice paying attention.

• • •

Holy Spirit, open the eyes of my heart to pay attention to the movements you are making in my own soul to clear out what must go for something beautiful to grow. Help me to hold curiosity and worship together. As I meditate on the touch of Jesus, draw me into worship. Father, forgive my constant state of hurry. Help me embrace the limits of my time and return time back to you as a gift.

Jesus, you are so beautiful. Help me to pay much closer attention to God, my soul, and the people you put into my path today. Amen.

8

THE GOODNESS OF
GATHERED SALT

An Invitation to Community

 confess that many of my first impressions of church ministry and marriage to a vocational pastor were formed by
the Christy Miller Series, the teen Christian romance novels
by Robin Jones Gunn. In my early teenage years, I'd fantasized
about marrying a boy like Todd, a blond surfer who would play
worship songs on a beat-up guitar on the beach. My one-day-
pastor boyfriend of my imagination would be a bit out of reach
because he was "seeking first God's kingdom." The romance
would take center stage and we could do all the churchy bits
on the side: mission trips, or small group ministry, or leading
youth group. I imagined that the church was what you did in
your small slices of time, not who you were.

Nearly twenty years into my marriage to an actual pastor (not a fictionalized one), we are both tethered tightly to the institutional and local church. This is a grace, because, as with many constraints, I sometimes want to run away.

Church is not something we do; it is who we are. When people from the neighborhood or church come over, our kids take a break from skateboarding and sit down in kid-sized beach chairs on our patio to talk. This isn't simply a string of events but something my children have been welcomed into: a hospitable life.

While as a young teen I thought marriage to a pastor might be more romance than work, as a younger pastor's wife I had hoped for the same romance surrounding church life. But after two decades of ministry, the sheen has worn off. What remains are not the wounds, wounds we've surely inflicted and wounds we've received—though they are there. Instead what lingers are those who have pressed in. They have seen our unshiny selves and stuck with us. What remains are the limits and gifts of community: the ones who cry and pray with us over cheddar and fig jam. The ones who show up, brokenhearted, in sweat-pants, in the midst of their own anxiety. The ones whose sorrows have laid them low and yet who bring all the tender pieces to Jesus.

These are the people who pray in the dark, who dig in with a motley group of people and choose to love anyway. This is the church.

• • •

The life of Christ was lived within the guardrails of Jewish faith and tradition. Jesus knew the Torah, he practiced Passover, he looked, ate, and spoke like a Jew of the first century. Since the Enlightenment, with our ideas about private property and private lives, we have become increasingly individualistic, favoring "me" over "we."

We have taken an eraser to our boundary lines in search of so-called freedom and happiness beyond constraints. Although our Christian pictures of Jesus often make him look Caucasian, a little bit like the blond surfer in my teen romance novels, and although we focus on our own experience of Jesus outside of his own cultural and religious context (thinking of Jesus as the pixie dust on a good, often Western, upwardly mobile life), his was a Middle Eastern, Jewish life.

We need to remember the very communal nature of Jesus' faith. Jewishness wasn't a tenet of belief so much as it was a way of life. Judaism provided a closed system in which an individual lived and moved. Money, time, attention, sexuality, work, and rituals were all encompassed by the communal and covenantal relationship of God with his chosen people. Judaism's Scriptures, traditions, rites, and ways of life—in short, its constraints— were the boundaries of a holy life. You couldn't find "your truth" outside of Yahweh making himself known to his people.

What Jesus offers to his disciples (and to us as recipients of the gospel to the ends of the earth) is more than an individual golden ticket to heaven when we die. He offers a long line of fulfillment of generational promises, of making a home for those burdened by slavery and exile, and fulfilling the promise to have a descendant of David on the throne. He not only keeps purification laws but teaches that the kingdom of God demands more, a new heart. He is prophet, priest, and king.

The freedom he offers is a collective freedom. He has come to prepare to marry his bride, the church.

We have lost something when we've made the Christian life all about going to heaven when we die and about an individual experience of God. While it is those things, it is more than that: Jesus fits us together, living stones on the foundation of Christ alone, and as our shepherd, guides us into spacious places not only for ourselves but also for the good of the world. He does so by taking in diverse individuals, calling us to follow him, and enabling us to practice community together.

> We are invited into the constraints of real community—with people who vote differently, and who look different and speak differently than we do—so that we all may be formed into something altogether new.

• • •

Curled up on our couch one night, I leaned forward as I watched Samin Nosrat eat. She chewed meat and looked longingly at ice cream. She ate tacos in Mexico, artisanal soy sauce in Japan, and fresh pasta in Italy in her Netflix documentary *Salt, Fat, Acid, Heat*. I wanted to eat like that, laugh like that, cook like that. She recommended that pasta water be as salty as the ocean as she dropped palmfuls into the boiling water.

Her cookbook by the same name breaks down each ingredient of good cooking. On salt, she says, "Salt has a greater impact on flavor than any other ingredient." But salt is also significant in other ways: "We need to consume it regularly in order to be able to carry out basic biological processes, such as maintaining proper blood pressure and water distribution in the body, delivering nutrients to and from cells, nerve transmission and muscle movement." Salt is not only vital for survival, but makes food delicious. It brings out flavor and it helps us do the work the body is designed to do.

In Matthew 5, in his Sermon on the Mount, Jesus teaches that God's presence is not limited by a temple or tabernacle. Rather than focus on a place as the locus of worship, the advent of the Son of God expands God's people and God's place—so now it is the wider people of God who are to be salt—to be a blessing to the nations. Jesus tells his listeners what the kingdom looks like: it is full of blessings for those who are peacemakers, who are persecuted, who are poor and meek. God has not forgotten the plight of his people. He reminds his hearers that they are "the salt of the earth"—their purpose is to provide saltiness to the earth (Mt 5:13).

Salt isn't very effective in single crystals. It needs to be gathered together to have any effect. We are to be scooped like handfuls of salt and tossed into water. We are to be a rub to tenderize meat. We are to be used to preserve the flavor and taste of food so it does what it's supposed to do—to help us work right, to nourish, and to delight. We're really not much use on our own. We don't do what we're supposed to do as lone rangers. God's people are gathered salt.

The purpose of salt is not to win awards, to catalog how amazing salt is. The purpose of salt is not to overwhelm a dish so the food is inedible. Neither is it to grow so stale or isolated that it's no longer useful. As Samin Nosrat reminds us, salt "has its *own* particular taste, and it enhances the flavor of *other* ingredients. Used properly, salt minimizes bitterness, balances out sweetness, and enhances aromas, heightening our experience of eating." The bit of sea salt on the top of fine chocolate makes the chocolate taste better. It makes it taste more like chocolate should taste.

The goodness of gathered salt is that it shows us how food works and tastes best. Might the people of God show us how we work best as humans—not overly individualistic, but bearing a communal identity of love? Might we be more concerned about enhancing the flavor of others than enamored with our own saltiness? May the people of God minimize bitterness, temper saccharine sweetness, and heighten the aroma of Christ. What does this look like? *Love. Joy. Peace. Patience. Kindness. Goodness. Faithfulness. Gentleness. Self-Control.* This is what we experience in such a gathered community.

> To be the gathered salt of God, we must consent to the constraints of community.

• • •

But to be the gathered salt of God, we must consent to the constraints of community—of being *for* others instead of using others—often through limiting our time, desires, and even those secondary identities we hold dear.

Before the coming of the Holy Spirit at Pentecost, those who followed Jesus were a rag-tag group of people mostly using Jesus for their own ends. Matthew was a despised tax collector who likely preyed on the poor and lined his own pocket. Simon was a zealot, an ardent nationalist, akin to a terrorist. Most were fishermen, many uneducated. Peter was married, some were brothers. A company of women followed too; some, like the women mentioned in Luke 8, Susanna and Joanna, provided financially for Jesus' ministry, and others only brought their need. Leaders came too, like Nicodemus, who was afraid of what others thought, so he met Jesus by night; but after Jesus' crucifixion, he was with Joseph of Arimathea to lay Jesus in a tomb.

Jesus' first disciples thought he'd be a Jewish Messiah they could understand: one who would secure their freedom, overthrow the Romans, reestablish the temple, and reassert the uniqueness of Israel as God's chosen people. How often do we too use Jesus for our own ends, for what he can offer us—a sort of sprinkle on top of our self-constructed lives?

Jesus does not abolish a communal life of the Jews for an individualistic, compartmentalized Western one. Jesus' life, death, and resurrection births the church—the people who he commissions and promises the Holy Spirit to—before he ascends to heaven. Jesus teaches and brings the kingdom of God to bear within place, within people, in order to form a people for himself. He builds a temple of people into the temple of his own body—often the marginalized, outcast, poor, and those who realize their deep need of him.

> Jesus invites us into the constraints of the church so we can live for the life of the world.

Jesus invites us into the constraints of the church so we can live for the life of the world.

• • •

I used to get comments at Costco all the time when my four children were very small (two in the cart, one strapped to me, and one walking alongside me): "Wow! Four! Are they all yours?" Often, I'd want to say something sarcastic ("No, I just grabbed a few off the street") or sweet but condescending ("My hands are busy, but my heart is full"), but generally I just smiled and nodded. "Yes, they're all mine."

Navigating the desires, wants, and needs of six of us means someone is often hurt, upset, angry, sad, lonely, or bored throughout the course of the day, and my husband and I simply can't meet everyone's needs at any given moment. I used to be angry at myself or my children for our lack of patience. When I began to embrace the limits of my time and attention, I began to see how our bigger family is a gift. My primary job is not to be the personal genie to each of my children but to show them how to navigate community.

While other children may have fewer squabbles (simply because they have fewer siblings) and might have more extracurricular activities offered to them, my children are learning how to belong to something greater than themselves or their personal happiness. They are learning young how the good life is not in freedom to do whatever you choose, whenever you want, but in creating a sustainable family that has a mission and purpose. To be a family means sacrifice, it means reckoning with disappointment, and it means their character is being formed. It also means there's a whole lot more laughter.

We say we want community, but we really like the feeling of community more than the work it requires. We expect community to do something for us, but we're rarely willing to sacrifice for it. Often we are unwilling to accept the constraints on our personal preferences for the good of our neighbor. But unless we do, we will not be living into the spacious life. We often opt for the latest self-improvement plan instead of being built into the house of God.

Rich community in the church, that first family that Jesus adopts us into—like a beef bourguignon or homemade pasta—builds and grows in its flavor only through constraints. It happens slowly. To build thicker communities, we'll have to stick around, live under gracious and loving authority, forgive each other, and choose to spend time together, rather than making the best choice for any one individual. Seth Kaplan writes: "In a North American context increasingly allergic to constraints imposed from beyond the self, there are fewer and fewer examples of the rich kinds of community we crave—few want to compromise their privacy and surrender their freedom." Rich community happens through diverse people, layered and simmering together.

We want the church to taste more like true community should taste. We crave the goodness of gathered salt. But to actually be the community we crave, we must limit ourselves. We limit ourselves by choosing to show up when at times we'd rather not. We limit ourselves when we give of our time to listen, talk, and pray. We limit ourselves when we participate in weekly liturgy even when we do not feel like it. We limit ourselves by giving our financial resources for the mission of the church. We limit ourselves by setting up chairs, or volunteering in children's ministry, or meeting with an elderly friend.

We limit ourselves by sharing not only ourselves but our very lives with those who are far from Jesus.

We choose constraints of our love: we send thank you notes or make a meal for neighbors. We offer to babysit the kids of a single mom or we show up for a church event even if it's not our "thing." We say hi to someone new on a Sunday and we ask the pastor a question about his sermon. We choose constraints on our resources: we tithe and give our money away. We choose to learn from others much different from us.

We choose constraints on our place, staying in community when someone votes, thinks, or acts differently than we do. These are the actions of the salty, gathered church.

Beautifully, we find that this is the economy of the kingdom, this is the way of Jesus: we give and find ourselves filled; we lose and yet find ourselves gainers of grace; we are weak but strong, weary but unashamed, and together we taste like Jesus.

As the years go by, we are being formed together, with Jesus as our gate, shepherd, and cornerstone, holding us all together.

I like to think of God sometimes as though he's at Costco, carrying all his children, carting us around. Some of us are joyful in the journey and others are falling apart, needing to be picked up and carried like a football under one arm. The onlookers stare. We're becoming the gathered children of God. Perhaps he smiles and tells someone, beaming: "Yes, can you believe it? They are all mine!"

• • •

Jesus, I know you were constrained for the sake of rescuing your people: Philippians 2 talks about you not counting equality with God something to be grasped but humbling yourself, even to death.

I confess I don't even want to rearrange my schedule for the people of God.

Forgive me for the ways I make all the problems of your people other people's faults. Convict and comfort me, O Spirit of God. Make the flavor of my heart and ways salty and delicious. Help me, God, to practice showing up for people, choosing to gather together with your people in life-giving communion with you and each other. Amen.

9

THE GIVENNESS OF THINGS

An Invitation to Remember the
Stuff of the Kingdom

*W*hen my parents remodeled their kitchen, they blocked in a small cabinet under the stairs to put in a small fridge in that space instead. This closet was the place I had claimed as my own, my own middle school prayer spot. The place I first met Jesus.

My parents laugh telling me how when they opened the closet before the remodel they found used matches and how they're thankful my candle-lighting there didn't burn down the house. It's funny (and relieving) to our adult ears.

But, as I recall, I had a small and cozy space to retreat to day by day. I remember lighting my candles and sticking the used matches back into an old matchbook and tucking them away under a wood shelf. I remember highlighting my Bible and journaling my prayers in a flowered notebook. I remember making checkmarks on Bible reading plans and struggling through hard-to-understand passages. Each day my candle and matches would delineate that space and time as holy: I'd strike my match then read, pray, and journal. These were the things that marked my growing relationship with Jesus, eager in its infancy.

We laugh at the matches now. Then, they were a witness.

• • •

Our relationship with stuff is complicated. We watch shows about how decluttering can spark joy, yet we are overrun with too many mugs, throws, or perfect white t-shirts, while others have too little. We think too little or too much of things.

We might prioritize the thing itself. Consider how a parent might blow up at a child when a porcelain canister lid is accidentally dropped and broken. The thing grows in importance disproportionate to its actual value (especially when compared to the child). Or we think of things as inconsequential: goods to consume, easily replaceable. So we purchase without thinking about the relational, economic, societal, or global cost.

But we are limited creatures. We need a proper relationship to our things—not so we can work at better controlling and ordering our lives but so we can stay connected to our unlimited God. We need the stuff of earth—like used-up matches—to witness to the work of God.

• • •

Things point to a Creator deeply concerned with the material world as a reflection of his beauty, truth, and goodness. And in our sin-soaked world, things too can be objects to mark redemption—even in our places of pain and betrayal.

I pause reading the story about Jesus washing his disciples' feet; I'm stuck on all the objects. The words are familiar, but I keep imagining the basin, water, and the towel, the bread and the wine, as Jesus marched toward his death.

While he was celebrating his final Passover meal with his disciples, Jesus took a towel and a basin and washed his disciples' feet. While usually a servant would do such a menial task, here their Lord does it. The basin, water, and towel were staples of the home—like a closet in which to place your coat and a table to hold your keys by the door.

The Passover meal too was full of ordinary elements—full of a liturgy and food the disciples knew by heart: unleavened bread, bitter herbs, wine. Yet in the hands of Jesus these symbolic elements that told the story of Israel's release from slavery were then instituted to become a sacrament for a new body of believers, bound not by ethnicity or circumcision but by the wide love of God.

> In the hands of Jesus, things find their proper use and place.

Bread and wine are more than bread and wine. Water, a basin, and a towel are more than mere cleaning items. They are vital elements of the gospel story, harbingers of the kingdom of God. In the hands of Jesus, things find their proper use and place.

These are the things that tell us we need to be washed and cleaned by Jesus and we need to feast on him if we are to have any part of him. They are things that remind us our primary identity is as washed and loved, as cleaned and sent ones. They invite us to do the same for others.

I can't shake the width and breadth of grace these things reveal. Jesus wrapped a towel around his waist and washed the feet of his disciples, even his betrayer. Jesus washed the muck off Judas's feet.

These redemptive, sacramental things were offered as a gift, even to a betrayer.

Peter wanted his whole body washed by Jesus and yet, at a fireside just hours after this meal, he denied even knowing Jesus. If Peter and Judas (and all his disciples—heck, all of us) can so easily reject the import of bread and wine, and yet these things can be effective means of grace, it means that the love that Jesus offers in and through them is bigger, more glorious, and more startlingly effective than we often think. Jesus makes things holy. And our response to the holy things he offers does not change their efficacy.

Because if Jesus can transform ordinary things, then he can also use these ordinary things to transform me. When I am in seasons of pain, I want to hold on to hurt like a hard and immovable thing—as if betrayals could be stacked up and revisited like a dragon's hoarded gold. But, in the hands of Christ, ordinary things are hallowed, and with them, he holds out redemption. When I receive these things, I am invited to open my hands. I too need washing. I too need to take and eat.

What if the things we have were neither something to orient ourselves around nor unimportant but instead—like our limits—invitations to knowing and communing with God?

Might things help us mark, watch for, and remember the work of God? So we begin to hunt for the ordinary things that show us the limitless love of Jesus.

• • •

I like to pick out Christmas ornaments on our travels: porcelain shoes from Holland, a taxicab from London. On a few fall days in the mountains, we visited a gift shop and I chose a wooden California grizzly bear with the name of the mountain town on it. My friend Karla picked out a few vintage-looking ornaments as we told the little ones to be careful and not to touch. This was our little mountain getaway with dear friends who had become family and ministry partners with us for nearly a decade.

Yet, this coming Christmas, they will put their ornaments on a tree in a new house across the country from us. We will put ours on a small tree I place on a table in a house where we will be guests, as we wait to see where we might land more permanently. The rhythms of this weekend are familiar from years of joint family getaways—the children run and play and jump in and out of the hot tub; Jason builds a fire and makes us coffee; my husband, Bryce, creates for us a feast, I pour the wine and we find ourselves deep in conversation under the stars. These rhythms are so familiar that I am lulled into thinking this is just another weekend with our friends.

But loss curls at the edges. This is the last mountain getaway before we part ways. How are we to do life well without Jason and Karla? If we stop for too long, the deep hollow growing in my chest might explode and I'll find myself weeping uncontrollably. So, we speak of future home renovations and the details of selling houses, of adventure, and our years of stored memories. I wonder how a small wooden Christmas ornament can stand in for all of that.

On the morning we pack up the Airbnb and take out the trash, we open *Every Moment Holy* to pray together. It seems fitting to pray prayers about journeying. We are headed into new places that promise rest and new work to do but that also require leave-taking and loss. Betwixt places that morning, with children moving between our limbs, we pray for prepared hearts "to revel in new exploration / of cities not our own / and of landscapes less familiar." I feel the weight of placelessness begin to press on my chest and the unraveling of what was. I can't stop the tears from flowing as we entreat our good God to "Bless our pilgrim quest for restoration!" *Please God, may it be so.* We are worn thin and weary. And yet, we feel our hearts burn again with longing—for all the hard to be redeemed and that all the good we experience now might simply be an appetizer to that kingdom feast. We look forward to a reuniting in "that best holiday celebration / that will one day / encompass all days, / and all of heaven / and all of earth."

So we drink our pumpkin coffees and buy our ornaments and say, "We'll see you soon."

A few days later in that tender space when the loss crashes in, I get a text from our dear friends in Utah, Mark and Melissa. A bottle of Utah rye whiskey is on its way. I think through the years of small things: eight years ago we held hot chocolate in our cold fingers and waited for Santa to come down the chair lift in Park City. I remember the red glass tea light holders that they have in Italian restaurants on the wooden table at Bar X, where Melissa and I might get a night of adult conversation. I recall red mugs of piping hot tea mixed with teary prayers while our children watched a show in the basement.

I think of how God's people took stones from the bottom of the sea when they crossed through it out of their slavery from Egypt. How they'd stack them as memorial stones, ebenezers, as a visual, tactile reminder of what God had done. Their children would ask and they'd tell them the thick, identity stories.

My bottle of Utah rye and my brown wooden bear are my memorial stones—testaments to God's faithfulness, that he provides companions for the journey even as we are not sure where it winds, and that his love knows no limit. I pack the wooden ornament away in its tissue paper and wait.

• • •

Things invite us to remember God's faithfulness, to mark time in sacred, not mechanistic, ways. I chew over the word *remember*—it isn't just recalling something or bringing it to mind. More than that, remembering involves our whole selves; to remember something involves making it a habit, retelling its story, reliving a moment or memory so that the past is actually brought into the present, so the past can even transform the present. As we remember, we are put back together, literally re-membered.

Two musicians, Andy Gullahorn and Gabe Scott, started a weekly high-five in 2014 to make sure these touring musicians and friends saw one another regularly. Walking thirty minutes between their homes, they'd meet for a high-five. A few years in, Gabe acquired a temporary version of encephalitis and lost his memory. Yet, in the hospital, when the now-stranger Andy asked him for a high-five, Gabe found his body responding as it always did with their signature clap, snap, high-five. Andy commented how the high-fives "built a safety net" for their friendship: "There's something about the aggregate of it that feels special. It's a commitment. It feels like an intentional waste of time, and I mean 'waste of time' in the best sense." Their weekly high-fives not only helped Gabe remember again but also helped put him back together. Something as small as a high-five can be a witness. With high-fives or wooden Christmas ornaments, we can mark redemptive time.

As we mark redemptive time in ordinary ways, we also re-member in sacrament. These too provide a safety net and take on significance in the aggregate. In the washing of Judas and in the Lord's Supper, Jesus showed how tangible things are instituted not as memorials to betrayal but as objects of redemption. Jesus looks us in the eyes too with our hands dipped in the bowl and invites us into a spacious life.

A spacious life is never about what you achieve or about the ways you haven't measured up; it is about an identity you are given. Washed. Forgiven. Beloved. A spacious life isn't about making sure you have the correct relationship to the stuff in your life, but it is an invitation to see things as memorial stones and markers of all things being made new.

The Lord's Supper helps us taste the love of God, a love that can swallow up pain and betrayal. This is our remembrance meal: here all things are made new. This is the meal Jesus said we were to do "in remembrance" of him (Lk 22:19). This is how we get grace inside us and how we get put back together week upon week.

Because the love Jesus offers in bread and wine, in body and blood, is the costliest meal in the universe, it widens the table so that all of us—self-righteous sinners and betrayers—can be welcomed in and covered. We are all in desperate need of the capacious love of Christ, a love that we can chew on and that glides down our throats.

The Lord's Supper points to a day when the crooked places will be made straight and all the rough places plain (Isaiah 40:4). Jesus told his disciples how he deeply desired to celebrate and eat this supper with them and how he wouldn't drink wine until they drink and sup together in God's kingdom on that final day.

> Because the love Jesus offers in bread and wine, in body and blood, is the costliest meal in the universe, it widens the table so that all of us . . . can be welcomed in.

So even now Jesus is fasting from the love feast until his bride arrives and we can all partake together. He waits still. Isn't that remarkable? That on the eve of his crucifixion, right as one of his disciples was in the process of betraying everything Jesus stood for, right as he told them how they'd all desert him and he would be alone, he was still desirous to celebrate. Why? Because this is our meal of love, our Eucharist, our thanksgiving meal, a sacrament that points to the reality of God's deep love for his people. Through this meal, we are put back together.

Christ's love not only swallows sin, death, and betrayal, it also robes us in his perfection. That means you're free to drink redemption in bread and wine; it also means you can begin to chronicle your own small, tangible memorial stones of God's redemption in your life.

I grasp in my hand a small wooden cross, a gift from a friend. I tuck it into my pocket to remind myself of the comforting presence of Christ. I pick seashells from the sand and send them in a box for a friend homesick for California. I mail a tea bag in a letter, hoping to provide a bit of calming presence. These are small things, but they are also memorial stones—personalized moments of God's redemption in time and space, stacked for others to see. From tea bags and high-fives to the bread and cup, these are the things that tell us who we are.

Take and eat. Take and drink. Stack your memorial stones and accumulate your high-fives. Let us wait well for the clink of glasses at the wedding feast.

• • •

Father, Son, and Spirit, Thank you for looking into the tender spots of weakness in my own heart and meeting it with your own limitless love. I open myself to you. Show me in small, tangible things how your kingdom is coming. Would you help me see things as heralds to your kingdom, messengers of grace, memorials to your faithfulness? Would you take away the sting of hurt and betrayal? Here I am, supple in your hands. May your Supper sustain and change me. May my limits always draw me to you. Amen.

10

PRACTICING THE
ART OF DYING

An Invitation to Abide

*W*e don't talk about it much," my husband said and squeezed my hand, "the baby that we lost."

The miscarriage was more than a decade ago and has been subsumed in the logistics of our now-full family: schedules, sports, church activities and dreams, my own writing and traveling to speak.

The pain was so fresh then. Now I work to remember. I remember sunlight streaming through double-paned glass, lighting up the white sheets on our bed. We had giggled at one another there. Here was new life, something we'd helped create. The future was bright and secure. I took photos each week, so I'd get to see my belly expand.

But with some early bleeding, I hurried to the doctor, hoping information would put my fears to rest. Walking home, I pulled my red wool coat tightly around my belly, dazed, the day gray. The pregnancy hormone in my blood was dropping, the doctor had said. The real bleeding started a few days later.

I sat over a cold toilet in midwinter as so much blood poured out—and wailed. Out of me came an unearthly, low, guttural howl. I rocked back and forth, and alternately gripped and pressed against the edges of the toilet seat—as if I could move away from the cramps and grief. I could only mouth the dagger words: "I hate myself," feeling as if my own body were responsible for the letting go.

Death had swallowed life and my body was the site where the drama was staged.

For months, the pain was fresh, something I tended. But now I wonder if there's something I need to mourn still. Had there been a door closed in my heart because I didn't keep one ajar for the child lost more than fifteen years ago?

This death reverberated in small ways I hadn't seen: now I weep for a little life gone. I cry for the ways I've protected myself, how playfulness is hard to come by, and the attending anxiety I carried into my other pregnancies. I wonder if that particular pain has boxed me into a smaller corner, where I sit, afraid to give my heart away again and be hurt, betrayed, or unnoticed.

Can we dive into pain and find God there? I know we say words as if we can, words about Jesus' own passion, but can we make a home in those words too? How do we keep wounds tender enough so they don't fester but also open enough so we are still deeply changed?

• • •

On the night he was betrayed, Jesus needed those who were dear: Peter, James, and John—the ones who reclined with him, who leaned against his chest and felt the heartbeat of God.

He asked them to stay close by while he prayed the prayer he didn't want to pray. His soul sinking already into the pangs of death, he offered small words to his friends: "Please, please stay. I'm sad and sorrowful and I know what I must do. But please, be close by. Please pray. Watch. Abide with me."

Walking a little bit away, his forehead in the dirt, he laid his body down before his Father. Primal groans burst from the deepest parts of himself. Was this the way it would happen? Couldn't redemption happen any other way? The words small and the sorrow wide. Hours he wrestled, he asked, he pleaded.

Later he came to his own: yet they were asleep. Frustrated, saddened, kind, he warned and encouraged them again—"Pray, don't fall into temptation"—words of pleading, words of warning. The aloneness enveloped him like the night sky. "Please friends, couldn't you please just stay awake with me? Will you love me that much? Please, please pray."

Again he went off to pray—bold, stark, truthful prayers: "Can this cup please pass? If there is any other way to save, I will do it. Will you let this cup pass from me?"

And then there was a sort of quiet resignation, a holy submission to the will of the triune God. Picking himself up off the ground of the garden, there was no other way. "My Father, if this cannot pass unless I drink it, your will be done. I will drink it down to the dregs."

The cup of sorrow and the cup of wrath. He drinks the cup of curses so that we can drink a cup of blessing. "Your will be done." He comes back to the ones he loved most. And they're sleeping again.

Is he overwhelmed with sorrow? Is he disappointed? Or is he kind enough to know they just need to sleep?

Yet this generosity increases his own deep aloneness. He prays again, rehearsing in his body the rhythm of placing his will under the will of the Father. A third time, he returns and they're sleeping. So he wakes them. Torches and the clanging of swords are coming. The hour is at hand—and he is alone.

• • •

When the days feel long and overwhelming, the emotions swirling and the pathway unclear, I take great comfort in the squeeze of my husband's hand under our bed covers. I can rest in that space because I have someone *with* me. We need to know we are not alone.

In the garden, Jesus was so very alone. His friends wouldn't pray with him, and soon he would also lose the face of the Father. That loss seemed like too much to bear. Yet through it all, he said yes to the Father's no. Jesus welcomes the no of God so we can always have his yes.

In our dark nights, we are invited not to numb or hide but to abide with Jesus. The word *abide* comes from English and Germanic roots meaning to stay put, to remain, even to wait defiantly, to stand ready, to sojourn, and to watch. Its past tense is *abode*, which is still used in its nominal form as a dwelling or house.

> Jesus welcomes the no of God so we can always have his yes.

Jesus shows us how to abide with God, to dwell in the Father like a house. The rhythms of our yes to God—how we abide with him—must be like his in the shadow of death: honest prayers that might be more groaning and listening than speaking, asking hard questions, and finally a yes to the will of God, trusting he will take care of us. This is the posture of entrusting ourselves to God. We all have known desolate spaces. Desolate spots of earth and deep caverns inside ourselves. Desolate seasons in our lives when we didn't know which way was up. We don't like them.

So instead of seeing our limits, naming them, and following our good guide where his rod and staff comfort us in the shadow of death, we construct our identities on things we can measure. We run away from loss and pain, we numb and we choose self-preservation instead of abiding with God and others.

When we acknowledge our limits and give them to God, we begin to look like Jesus. We recognize our deep need for others and the voice of God the Father. In the Garden of Gethsemane, Jesus does what our first parents failed to do in the first garden: Jesus finds a home for his desires and will within the limits of his loving Father. He abides pain and he abides with the Father even through death, even through desertion, when his disciples failed to remain. Even with impending pain, the aloneness of the cross, the existential weight of sin crouching at his door, Jesus chose to limit himself because of love.

Jesus limits his autonomy for the salvation of the world.

Jesus limits his autonomy for the salvation of the world.

• • •

There's a phrase I can't quite put down: *ars moriendi*, the art of dying. I found it in *The Keys to Bonhoeffer Haus* written by my friend, Laura Fabrycky. I like the way it sounds. That which we push off with our millions of distractions—death—might instead be an invitation, and it has an art attached to it. Death might be a sort of comma before a new phrase, instead of a grim reaper ready to take away all we've ever known.

In her book, Laura Fabrycky asks us to see Dietrich Bonhoeffer's life as a "masterpiece in the art of dying," as *ars moriendi.* The Latin phrase originated with handbooks on dying in the fifteenth century; they were useful for laypeople if a priest could not get to the dying's bedside in time. In these handbooks, the Christian was admonished to resist particular temptations: the temptation against faith, the temptation to despair, the temptation to be impatient, to succumb to vainglory or pride, as well as the temptation to avarice. Put another way, each admonishment against temptation was an invitation to virtue: to keep faith, hope, patience, and humility, while also detaching from possessions and reputation as one lay dying.

The art of dying well rejected running away from loss into the seemingly safe landscape of self-preservation. Instead, abiding with Christ—as Jesus' own disciples failed to do in Gethsemane—means embracing loss, embracing the unknown, and moving through pain. As Fabrycky writes, these handbooks for the dying "offered the hope that a path of life wound even through the valley of death." While we desire to abide with Christ in our final breaths, we also practice abiding with him in both our everyday and more tragic losses.

As we learn to abide with Christ through loss and suffering, keeping watch in prayer, our muscle of hope grows. So then, we practice going *through* pain rather than around, under, or over it.

This is the story of the Bible: that God is love and that this God of the cosmos is our great lover who will stop at nothing, not even death, to win for himself his lost people. He will bring them home. While we might take that sentence and put it up like a pendant on the wall to say which team we belong to, when faced with big and small deaths day by day, we live what more often feels like a cramped life through endless achieving rather than a more spacious one. We're more apt to go to the grave grasping our hustle to prove we're worthy and our hurry to show we're enough, rather than abandon ourselves to a good God who whispers that death is the pathway through.

Going through pain might look like letting yourself feel your feelings. It may look like crying, angry outbursts, long exercise sessions where you shout at God, or small breath prayers in the midst of depression. Can you choose to not run from your limits or your pain and stick with Jesus instead all the way through?

Might your limits be the very thing that God chooses to use, the thing that God uses to press in close to whisper he will never leave? When you choose to forgo sleep to accomplish more, or lie about your mental illness, or not listen to your body, when you try to do too much in the hopes of being worthy of love, you miss out on this invitation.

Your limits are an invitation into the presence of God. He desires to meet you in your limits.

Jesus invites you to bring your limits to him, to lay the spinning plates down at his feet and hear the very yes of God. We utter a thousand small yeses with how we spend our days: in the choice to immerse ourselves in the story of God rather than taking the news as gospel truth, doing the hard work of relational repair, breathing before responding, giving away our time and money when we'd rather spend them on ourselves, choosing the present moment over a nostalgic backward glance or covering the future with self-enacted grand plans. It happens as we give away our privilege for those without a voice. It happens as we choose to gather, pay attention, and rest in this crazy paradox: our limits are an invitation to know God and make him known.

. . .

What if we were to experience a different story of *ars moriendi?* If we know that the story of the gospel winds even through death (not just Jesus' death, but our own dark spaces), then the small deaths to our ego or the larger, incomprehensible losses are all invitations to abide with Christ—not only in his sufferings, but for him to abide with us in ours. We are invited into the art of abiding.

Abiding connotes watchful paying attention, staying put; as mentioned, its past tense, *abode*, also calls to mind another word for house. The word *abide* also interestingly, has roots in the sixteenth century connected to "atoning for," used in Milton's *Paradise Lost.*

In book four of *Paradise Lost* we find Satan, the fallen angel, contemplating his task to lure Adam and Eve into sin. He remorsefully notes how though he is enamored in hell, yet he now must abide, or atone for, his boast about desiring omnipotence like God: "Ay me!," he cries, "They little know how dearly I abide that boast so vain." While Satan must atone for his sin by abiding it, we are invited to a different house, a different abode.

Because Christ abides the stain of sin, we are welcomed into the abode of God's love. Christ's abiding frees us from our own need to atone for ourselves and offers us a welcome mat: we may simply abide, waiting and watching for what God is up to.

> **Because Christ abides the stain of sin, we are welcomed into the abode of God's love.**

The invitation here is to remain, to stay housed in the abode of Jesus' own body through pain and deep aloneness. It is to recognize the way sin has twisted our desires and habits, how we are apt to run from our limits instead of letting them be sheltered inside the house of God.

In a hard season of ministry, my husband and I took deep comfort in this word *abiding*. Our call wasn't to fix the problems, or change people, or even work on a campaign of self-improvement. Instead it was simply to "hold fast." We are not called to change the world or work ourselves into a more virtuous form of ourselves. We are simply called to lean into our limits, trusting Christ will remain with us. We are called to remain faithful; we are called to stay.

Staying might be the hardest thing to do when in moments of profound loss we too want to chastise ourselves, or push away from the pain, to point dagger words at ourselves to try to atone for loss and suffering. Yet, know this: even when we fail to lean into the pain, we can trust our good Shepherd to go ahead of us, knowing he abides with us still.

Let us allow the losses to sink to the pit of our stomachs: the bloodied Christ gasping for air goes there with us. He knows the heart of evil. He knows what shame tastes like. He feels the severing of limbs, the disintegration of body, mind, and soul, and the words he chooses on the cross are the deep formative words of Scripture. Jesus chooses to give up life itself to welcome us into the abode of love.

And when we have the yes of a love that abides with us even in deep darkness, we find we are never alone. A more spacious life opens up in the valley of the shadow of death. When we follow in the way of Jesus, we are offered peace even in turmoil, abiding presence even in despair, hope even in darkness.

It is this moment—in the body of one Middle Eastern Jewish man on a cross, on a hill outside the city of Jerusalem— that we are welcomed into a more spacious life.

Here is the door! Will we enter in? He is the gate, the entrance into abundance; indeed, he is more than the entrance into the spacious life: Jesus is the spacious place itself. Abide with him, knowing he abides with you.

• • •

Jesus, I cannot comprehend your death. You were mocked, went into the wilderness outside the city gates to take on a death to bring a people into your love. You have gifted me with the very yes of God. Would you help me count my losses? Let me name them now.

I admit I'm fearful of death. I don't want to die, and I don't want to die to my plans or ideals. I'm afraid I'll be eradicated, invisible, and forgotten if I let go.

Yet, I'm trusting that you are the bread of life and that you will never let me go. Would you be with me as you lead me even through the valley of the shadow of death? Would you give me faith to embrace the life you have for me, give me courage to say yes to all the countless small deaths of self, so that what is borne in me is your real, abundant life? I want real life. God, how I want a spaciousness of soul so I am unafraid, unselfconscious, and content. Would you grow that small seed in me, please? Abide with me, Lord Christ, through the watches of the night. Amen.

11

FOLLOWING THE
GUARDRAILS OF LOVE

An Invitation to Be Surprised by Hope

O ne fall day in Utah, we loaded up our two small boys in our Subaru to chase the fall colors. The drive through the canyon was beautiful but we wanted more striking reds, more golds to take our breath away, so we continued up the narrow mountain road. We noticed winter had begun this high up. My boys thrilled at the snow! I marveled and tightened the seatbelt around my pregnant belly. The road became smaller, wide enough for a car to pass only if we pulled over with our wheels hugging the side of the mountain edge. It seemed a bit precarious without a guardrail. We noticed a few cars stuck in the unexpected early snow, but we continued on. There was fall to document and winter to find.

Yet a mile later we realized we'd surely share the same fate of these stuck cars and needed to turn around. But we couldn't find an area wide enough for a three-point turn. We slipped and slid, my husband deftly using the hand brake. When we found a small turnout, we proceeded to turn around through fits and starts. I gripped the seatbelt and prayed we would make it when it felt like our wheels were spinning and we'd get stuck. I gave my toddler boys a look so searing they knew to be quiet so my husband could concentrate on the task at hand. I tried to not think about our rear wheels falling off the edge of this unguarded mountain road and all of us falling to our deaths. I clawed into the seat with silent prayers and deep breaths as my husband cautiously and carefully kept us from falling down the side of the road and kept our wheels from digging too deeply into the snow.

As we finally were headed down the road, I remembered to breathe normally again and, for the sake of my two small boys, didn't mention the terror I felt. But I was shaken. Without guardrails on that road to contain us, it felt entirely possible that we could have tumbled down a cliff.

I thanked God for preserving us, for my skilled husband, and for the solid, flat highway, complete with guardrails, as we drove home.

• • •

We think guardrails restrict our freedom. When freedom is freedom from constraints, we live in a world we control—yet we find ourselves caged by the things we chase.

Good guardrails protect us from falling off the side of the cliff and also allow us space to play, explore, and even fail, knowing we are secure. Creativity flourishes amid constraints. A friend of mine had a college art course in which her professor allowed students to use just two complementary colors the entire semester. Rather than shutting down her creativity, it allowed it to expand. Limits also help provide stability that lessens anxiety. Sissy Goff writes about allowing an anxious child to ask her caregiver the same sort of worry question only five times a day; the child learns to turn off her "worry brain" and to slow down and think, which has the added effect of teaching her to self-regulate her own feelings. These guardrails don't take something from us, they actually bestow on us the necessary constraints for flourishing.

The problem is somehow in our gut we often don't think God-given limits allow for flourishing. We need something as drastic as resurrection to wake us up. James K. A. Smith writes: "If freedom is going to be more than mere freedom *from*, if freedom is the *power* of freedom *for*, then I have to trade autonomy for a different kind of dependence. Coming to the end of myself is the realization that I'm dependent on someone other than myself if I'm going to be finally free." Dependence, not independence, is the pathway into a more spacious life.

But "coming to the end of myself" can look more like despair than hope. I sat on the couch one morning, a cup of tea in my hands and a candle lit. As we prepared to move, the house got barer and barer. Our home mirrored our souls: all the clutter was being cleared out. The silence was thick. It felt like we were waiting in an in-between space; it made me think of Holy Saturday, the day between the crucifixion and resurrection, the day that A. J. Swoboda calls "awkward," a "holy day to sit, wait, and hope, unsure of what is to come." I felt both upheld by a hope that God would be good and faithful to us and also completely at a loss about the details.

People told us how courageous we were following God into the unknown, but instead it felt as if we were living in a dream, waiting and walking like Abraham, to see the land God would show us. I did not feel particularly remarkable, faithful, or spiritual. I didn't know what exactly I should be looking for or how to know it when "it" came. All I knew to do during this prolonged Holy Saturday was to sit, wait, and hope.

• • •

No one expected the resurrection. Yet, early Sunday morning, Jesus began to breathe again. He surprised Mary in the garden. Her heart became whole with her name spoken by a voice she knew so well: "Mary."

> Darkness is always transformed by intimacy.

Darkness is always transformed by intimacy. She ran, flung herself at him: "Teacher!" She ran to report to the disciples. She was the first evangelist to the good news: Even death has died! Everything sad will come untrue!

Later that day two disciples had already left the company of the bruised and brokenhearted band of Jesus-followers and begun the long walk home to Emmaus. They met the risen Christ on the road but supposed him a fellow traveler. It's the dejected note in their greeting that made Jesus' resurrected presence all the more tender.

Jesus asked, "What are you talking about?" Looking downcast, Cleopas incredulously responded, "Are you the only visitor in Jerusalem who doesn't know what's happened?"

Putting words to his pain and deep disappointment, he told the traveler of Jesus of Nazareth: "But we had hoped that he was the one to redeem Israel."

"But we had hoped." These too are our words.

And so Jesus the traveler walked with them, the sad, bruised, and broken ones, and opened up the Scriptures, reframing the law and the prophets and showing how it was "necessary that the Christ should suffer these things and enter into his glory" (Lk 24:26). All the way through—from the Garden, to the law at Sinai, to the prophets—Jesus showed them how all of it pointed to himself.

When it was night, the travelers asked their companion to stay. But then the guest became the host, and when he broke the bread, suddenly their eyes were opened. What was irrevocably broken was knit together and grew before their eyes. It was Jesus! Eating a meal with them! Alive! The devastation of hope had been turned inside out and made into an entirely new garment.

Rehearsing their joy, they recount: "Did not our hearts burn within us while he talked to us on the road, while he opened to us the Scriptures?" (Lk 24:32). Didn't we have glimmers of knowing, even then? How the bread made him known, how he as host was broken and given. So they ran the seven miles back to the room of scared and fearful disciples to testify to the hope that had filled up all the cracks of longing and belonging.

• • •

No one expected a Messiah like Jesus. No one expected the Messiah to die, to defeat the powers of death and hell through death, and no one expected the resurrection. The Gospel stories show us a cacophony of surprised and incredulous followers. How could this be? But yet it *is*.

Until Love himself breaks in, we have no imagination for resurrection. We must be "grasped by what we cannot grasp," held by what we cannot hold. And when we, the limited ones, are grasped by the grace of the unlimited One, there we find surprise: the surprise of hope.

Until Love himself breaks in, we have no imagination for resurrection.

The resurrection brings the reality of future hope into our present, small, embodied lives. N. T. Wright says it like this: "Easter was when Hope in person surprised the whole world by coming forward from the future into the present." Jesus meets the despair of Mary and the dejection of the disciples on the road to Emmaus. He surprises them with a future, cosmic hope that undoes their despair. But Hope also pulls up a chair and sits with them in their actual, ordinary lives—where they walk home or find a quiet spot to cry in the garden.

Our imaginations, like theirs, are stunted, limited to the ways and workings of God. We need the surprising hope of resurrection to meet us right in our dishwashing and studying, in our fighting and our despair, in our walking and mourning. Right in the middle of our preening and posturing and regular overwork where we ignore the limits of our time, bodies, affections, and calling.

We want resurrection power to look grand, feel flashy, and provide an emotional high that transforms the ordinary into glory. Resurrection can be spectacular. Yet, as we follow the lives of the disciples, we find that resurrection is also an invitation to a surprising hope. This hope often looks small and ordinary: a garden, a conversation, someone walking with them on the road, bread and wine.

So now in my empty living room I practice praying for surprise, longing to be met by a traveler who comes to bring "news from a country we have never yet visited," a place we will know when we see it. He is a man who dignifies the ordinary, pointing to signposts on the road to resurrection. My task is not to read the tea leaves to discern God's handiwork but to remain within the guardrails he's given. This is the invitation to hope.

• • •

How might we open up space for an imagination that can still be hopeful without being Pollyanna-ish? How might we cultivate hope?

It's said that farmers in the Great Plains have frozen to death just feet from their back door. Getting turned around in snowy blizzard conditions, they became disoriented between the barn and home. So many farmers tied a rope from the house to the barn, something tangible to hold onto, a lifeline between places that would anchor them and would bring them safely home. This is their guardrail. It limits their movement and freedom, yet without it they would die. The limitation of the rope is actually the very thing that provides life.

Our limits too are not strictures holding us back but doorways into intimacy with God. I wonder too if it is only as we acknowledge and embrace the goodness of our limits that we can embrace hope. Those who control and cajole, who court approval and fame, who must keep performing to be loved, often remain mired in cynicism with stunted imaginations that cannot go beyond what they cannot understand.

Grace upends. Resurrection surprises. Beauty remakes us.

I found some of this surprising hope break through during our season of being in-between, staying in a temporary home. There was art on the walls that caused me to catch my breath. I bent down to look closely at one, to ponder how Mary and Jesus have a halo in an abandoned gas station. I enjoyed the feel of the wood planks under my feet, the way the Persian rugs felt against my toes. I curled up in front of a fireplace with a tartan blanket and a cup of tea, listening to the crackle of wood and flame. I wrote letters for the first time in ages. I tucked my children into bed with big, downy comforters. Even the air conditioning vents were beautiful. I didn't have any long-term answers, but I had this moment of beauty. I hadn't known how starved for beauty and rest I'd been, but when it appeared, I cried, finding myself welcomed back into a country from which I had been long estranged.

But of course we are not all the way home yet; we are on the way. So we wait, we walk, and we cultivate hope in the ordinary ways Jesus gives us. We hold ourselves lightly and our plans loosely, anticipating surprise, expecting resurrection. Because this is the new way of things. I hold on to ropes of Scripture, repeating them as I feel anxiety rise. I spontaneously ask my children or husband to pray with me. While I'd thought a week or so off church attendance might feel like a lovely reprieve, I now know I might drown if I gave that up. These are not my strictures; they are my guardrails, my rope to bring me home.

When I was in a moment of despair in the emptying house, I remember blowing out a candle and how the scent of the wax and smoke took me back to my grandmother's Methodist church with its uncomfortable white wooden pews and formal liturgy. She would offer to take me to children's Sunday school during the service, but I always stayed by her side. I see now how long the road of faith is. How, even as a child, I have been hemmed in and led, given good guardrails to follow, so that now I know what ropes to reach for, which ropes will steady me.

• • •

The resurrected Christ meets us in ordinary places in ordinary times through ordinary means. He calls our names like he called Mary's. Jesus let Thomas stick his hand in his wounds and he walked and talked compassionately on the road to Emmaus. He invites us to simply walk on the way with him. He meets us in our dejected despair on the road. He meets us in our incredulity and stiff-arming, he meets us in our sadness, and he meets us in our waiting. We are free to bring our limited selves to Jesus, knowing hope has the last word.

> The resurrected Christ meets us in ordinary places in ordinary times through ordinary means.

Let us practice limiting our cynicism and control, our contempt and the supposition that if we just *knew* more, we would *be* more. We are free to bring our real, dejected, limited selves to Jesus. Like beloved children, we are empowered to hope even when the way is dark, knowing we have a good guide who has gone this way before.

Resurrection invites us to hope, not just for ourselves but for our work in the world. Our limits then, aren't like limps holding us back but gifts of self-restraint to steward. Christ, the only man who was truly free, limited his freedom so that he could give it away in love. We too, enrobed in that love, are invited to love God and love others—not despite our limits but through them.

Let us tend to small things. We change the sheets, we do our work, we encourage a friend, we bring a meal, we follow in the guardrails of faith. We practice limiting our so-called freedom for the flourishing of others—even in the meal made, the dishes done, the plants watered, and the tax returns filed. Jesus, the man of hope, will meet us there. This too is enough. Here there is room enough for hope.

• • •

Lord God, When confronted with my limits and a woefully small imagination, it's easy to turn to despair and see only myself. Lord Christ, transform the muscles of my soul to tell of your goodness, even to retell that story to myself. Give me courage to do the small things that tell of resurrection and allow others to journey with me on the road as we hold on to your guardrails. May my limits be how I love you and others. May your hope surprise and uphold me. Amen.

12

SOME SUPERHEROES
CLEAN TOILETS

An Invitation to Purpose

*a*t age twenty-seven, I pumped breastmilk in the ladies'
bathroom during fifteen-minute breaks. Slumping on
the tile floor and surrounded by beige metal doors, I thought
about my baby, upstairs in a hotel room with my mom, while
my husband and I spent four days in the conference center
rooms below. We'd flown across the country for a weekend
of church planting assessment through our denomination.
We had interviews and meetings, team exercises, and meals
together—and frankly the quiet moments in the bathroom
were a reprieve. Just the whirr-shush of the breast pump and
a cold floor.

Tethered by body and affection to our child and to what seemed our bright future, I thought I could do it all. Or at least I would try. I had, after all, managed to grade college papers with my infant curled beside me and a dog at my feet. So in the bathroom I pumped for my baby, and outside those doors I answered questions, talked about personality profiles and the goodness of the gospel, made conversation, and worked in teams.

We had our next step lined up: we were going to apprentice with a church in Portland and then go on to plant a city center church. We bought North Face gear to fit in. Our purpose was clear, our path laid out, and we couldn't wait to get started with our "real work."

We flew home, exhausted in body and soul, and our infant son screamed the whole plane ride. I shooed away help. I would meet his needs, bouncing him in the back of the plane with him swaddled and me swaying. We looked a sort of drunk duo, stumbling in the galley, desperate for quiet. I ignored the stares. I could not do it all.

Shortly thereafter, the Portland option fell apart. We were left jobless, without direction, and too many questions for God who didn't seem to answer. What was our purpose when it all came undone?

• • •

After the resurrection, Peter and a few disciples returned to their boats and nets. In the east as dawn broke, Jesus stood on the shore. "Have you any fish?" he called. They hadn't. Weary and exhausted, they had nothing to show for their labor. He told them to put the nets on the other side and suddenly, they were full of more than a hundred wriggling fish! This is Jesus, John realized!

Peter, our man of quick action, put his tunic back on and threw his body out of the boat to swim one hundred yards to shore. The fire crackled. The smell of charcoal and fish grilling made their stomachs growl. Jesus had hunks of bread too. "Come and eat breakfast," he said. "Bring some of that fish you just caught."

They sat there on the shore. A warm quiet came over them as they settled into the morning light, cold sand, and the warmth of the fire, like they were finally home. But Peter's heart thumped loudly; he remembered the anguish of regret. His own betrayal. He had left Jesus, said he didn't even know him.

Jesus looked at Peter, his eyes true and steady: "Simon, son of John, do you love me more than these?" Peter's heart dropped, its eagerness punctured: "Yes, Lord; you know that I love you." "Feed my lambs," came the reply.

Again Jesus asked, "Simon, son of John, do you love me?" Again Peter responded, grieved. Love was, after all, all he had left, even if it was weak: "Yes, Lord; you know that I love you." "Tend my sheep," the command.

And again, for the third time, Jesus asked, "Simon, son of John, do you love me?" Peter's heart was broken open: "Lord, you know everything; you know that I love you." "Feed my sheep," Jesus said (Jn 21:15-17).

Each word both a wound and a salve.

Three times by the fire before Jesus was tried in the middle of the night, Peter's eagerness and love for Jesus had been questioned. Each time he hid in the shadows. Now Jesus served him breakfast, providing for the bodies and tiredness of the disciples. And three times again, Jesus asked Peter about his love. But each time Jesus responded by giving him a task, good work to do: feed, tend, shepherd.

Jesus restored Peter. He took him from hothead, glory-seeking, full-throttle disciple and held a mirror up to his treachery. But instead of shame, he offered clarity. He made a hot breakfast. While he gave Peter good work to do—to pastor, tend, and feed the sheep of God—he made it clear: Jesus is the good shepherd. And he welcomed Peter into the beautifully broken way of grieving his sin, repenting, and coming broken-hearted and bellyaching to Jesus.

And with his mouth upturned, Jesus said, *Now, Peter, now you have good work to do. Follow me.*

• • •

Maybe like me, you've thought of yourself as needing to "do it all"—or at least meet your potential—to be noticed, loved, or respected. Maybe you felt invisible if you weren't achieving or setting goals; or, when you've failed, you were bent down with shame like Peter. Maybe you've thought of purpose and mission (like identity) as something to *achieve* instead of *receive*.

But when we achieve our identity and achieve our purpose we bypass our limits and usually run over or sidestep people in the process. More work is needed to keep measuring up and more shame comes to try to atone when we fail. We are used to living the unlimited life of production, achievement, and measurable results. We work for our identity: we bounce a baby on our own with too little sleep, we do not ask for help, we do not extend ourselves for the good of our neighbors. Our paid and unpaid work cannot hold up our identity formation.

Some Superheroes Clean Toilets

Friend, when our hustle runs out or the hurry exhausts, Jesus is kindly bringing us to the end of our rope, so we don't have to keep running any longer. He's serving us breakfast on the beach. Our limits, then, aren't what bar us from Jesus; they are an invitation into love.

> When our hustle runs out or the hurry exhausts, Jesus is kindly bringing us to the end of our rope, so we don't have to keep running any longer.

And within the guardrails of Jesus' love, he invites you, like Peter, to do good work. If you think the mercy of God has passed you by, that you, like Peter, are unable to do the good work God requires, Dane Ortlund tells us this good news: "The evidence of Christ's mercy toward you is not your life. The evidence of his mercy toward you is his—mistreated, misunderstood, betrayed, abandoned. Eternally. In your place." We can stop reading our present circumstances to try to work out God's pleasure.

Jesus restores us to good work not to give us an opportunity to earn favor but, because we already have his favor, to restore our purpose. He is like a father who invites his child to file papers or swing a hammer alongside of him—to delight together in the work the father is already about.

Work, then, begins to look different. We are not to whitewash our work with religious paint but to do our work in the Jesus way. Our limits help us get curious about what God is already doing. Work becomes just one way in which we glorify God and practice enjoying him, like the shared shoulder-to-shoulder work of a father and son.

Jesus gives Peter small verbs: *tend* and *feed*. When we tend or feed, we do not create the food or the conditions for flourishing. We simply use what is already there. We create safe places for others. We serve meals. We offer to others what has already been offered to us. We are witnesses, not creators. We are fellow pilgrims, not God's CEOs.

• • •

For years, I fought against the limits of my life. I chafed under the disconnect between what I imagined life would be and what it was. I felt tied down by moves and maternal duties, wondering what good a PhD was when I spent my days and nights half-awake, my body the site for an infant's pilgrimage. I wanted a story tied with a bow, with jobs materializing after years out of the academy, or a fast ticket to authorial success. This would be the good life, if I could have all my early dreams about calling and vocation gifted back to me.

I've since learned that the gift of those years wasn't a someday future success but the long slow work of finding beauty and purpose in ordinary elements. They brought me to the end of my talent, to the end of my limits—often hourly. Working through the phases of grief, stealing a few minutes alone in the bathroom, choosing to commit words to a page no matter what they would get me—these were the slow motions of belonging to a wider more spacious place where I was not the one in charge.

Part of our work as followers of Jesus is resisting the limit to create our own purpose and instead to receive the one God gives us, even if it doesn't look like what we imagined. My children were not inconveniences to more important things; they named the boundaries of my body and the limits of that season of mothering little ones. So, eventually, I found I could press into that change, acknowledge the tiredness of my mind and body, cry out about weariness of soul, and ask my wider community for help.

Our limits not only invite us to participate in God's work in the world but also show us how purpose is not an individual pursuit. Jesus, who limited himself for love, asks us to follow him: to steward our limits for others. Limits create conditions for community.

A friend from church, herself a mother of four, texted me when I came home from the hospital with my fourth child. She told me she would be coming over in a few days to scrub my bathroom toilets. It sounded too gross, especially with three boys, one of whom was starting to potty train. It seemed too much, and dare I say, too extravagant a gesture. Yet I knew my weariness from my daughter's stay in the NICU, and how my husband and I simply could not do something even as small as cleaning toilets. And they needed cleaning.

We texted, "Thank you! Yes please!" because we knew our limits. And we knew that the wider love of Jesus meant that our limits invited others in to share that burden. Our vulnerability opens doorways to tangible acts of mercy and care.

Purpose needn't be grand. When we practice growing curious about what God is already up to, there is a lightness about the work we do (and the work we receive). We're simply doing what we're called to as part of the family business. We're swinging our hammer. Our good work to do finds its home when we see all our work as holy—and as something we all do together.

• • •

The superhero myth persists—especially for women. We believe we should somehow be able to do it all and have it all: the high-powered career, the marriage and family, the community and church involvement, while staying fit and fashionable. Yet the type of work Jesus invites us to is received rather than earned. It is where all our work and all our lives, as it is given back to God, is worship.

This flies in the face of our myth of disconnected achievers. "Mothers—like fathers, like children, like every human being—aren't made for autonomy, even the autonomy that parades like courage and selflessness. Heroism is not required for making life work," Jen Pollock Michel reminds us. "*Dependence* is." If we do not honor our limits, trying to act the superhero instead, we will leak out dysfunction on those around us. In trying to do more or be more, we will become short-tempered, flattening people into objects or inconveniences. We will fail to stretch and grow and do the hard work of community building, preferring instead to do only that which brings praise, love, success, or notice.

Our limits show us that we need others, and our limits point us to good work God has for us not as superheroes but as servants. Our limits lead us into God's good purposes.

• • •

Jesus gave Peter back his purpose on the beach that morning, even after betrayal, even after he'd gone back to his fishing nets. The limits of his personality, temperament, zeal, or action did not bar Peter from mission. Rather, his humility and the resurrection of Jesus and the later coming of the

Holy Spirit guided Peter into work that wasn't simply for him but for others.

Our purpose has less to do with what we do and more to do with who we are becoming in Christ. Peter's limits drew him deeper into the love of Christ, made him more dependent on the power of the Holy Spirit to effect change, and more compassionate about the failings of others.

When Adam and Eve transgressed their first limits, choosing instead to find a path to flourishing outside of God's loving care, work became toil. They contended with thistles and thorns. One of their sons killed another.

> Our purpose has less to do with what we do and more to do with who we are becoming in Christ.

Yet with the resurrection of Christ and his ascension, with the coming Holy Spirit, work is redeemed—not fully of course, but we see glimpses of work as partnership. For work to not rule over us, we are invited to both accept the work God has for us and to put limits around the work we do. Work becomes just one way we live out our purpose: "to glorify God and enjoy him forever."

We are invited like Peter on the beach into our work as something tangible that evidences our deeper restoration. Work flows out of a greater purpose. So, as we go about our work, we are free to name our limits: we may not have a particular skill or personality, we are tired or weary, we need help. Our limits form the contours of doing good and faithful work because they help us to continually pay attention to God—the one who authors all good things. We just do our small part, we tend tasks and shepherd people as he calls us.

When my husband stepped down from a ministry role, it was to courageously name a limit: we could not keep going at the sprinting pace we'd been going for the last several years. It would have been detrimental to our marriage, family life, and the way we see God leading us to love and care for others inside and outside the church.

> Our limits form the contours of doing good and faithful work because they help us to continually pay attention to God.

Naming and acting on that limit looked like courage from the outside, but from inside it felt like death or, at times, a weird sort of floating. Plunged into the unknown where everything we imagined hadn't come to pass. Dreams were burrowed deep and we prayed they were seeds God would choose to grow someday. Yet, purpose is bigger than a job or work we do. It is a response to our received identity—even when it doesn't pan out or we burn out.

We practice telling ourselves the better story: our purpose is more than what we do. Our work does not define who we are. No matter how we or our work are received, we are upheld by the very grace of God. We become a still spot in a turning world—even as we wait, or groan, or do not know which way to turn.

We are colaborers and witnesses to God, the tender of the vine and that great shepherd of the sheep. We live into our called purpose as enjoyers of God in our small, caretaking disciplines: through prayer, Scripture reading, drinking water and eating healthy food, playing games with our family, going for walks, enjoying good meals with friends, participating in worship.

It is God's land to cultivate how he sees fit, not ours. So whether he calls me to clean someone's toilet, to write a book, to fold the laundry so my husband can apply for jobs, to bend down and tell a child again how they're capable of making their own sandwich, or to tell someone about the spacious life Jesus offers us, these are all my small verbs of kingdom living.

Each moment, the limits of my time, attention, place, desires, and passion can be given back as a gift to the One who has brought me out into a spacious place because he delights in me. He gets to decide what matters. Only he knows what small action, what tentative and helpless prayer, will ripple through generations. In his economy, we are not sure which works will bear a bounteous harvest and which will be chaff. This lifts the burden of needing to endlessly parse which work is worthy of our time. We are called to a greater purpose—like Peter, to sit with Jesus. We are called to tend and to feed. We practice curiosity about what God is already doing.

As we consider our own limits, and the work that we do, are we more concerned with achieving something for ourselves than in participating in the kingdom of God?

But if we see our own limits are gifts, we are hemmed in by God's covenant faithfulness on both sides. As we endeavor to keep walking in the guardrails of faith, a spacious life will grow, bit by bit, inside us.

Here is freedom. Here is the good life. Not in more but in less. Here we find that although the spacious life Jesus offers looks small and homely, the inside is bigger than the outside. Inside it you have nothing to prove. Inside you can wear the garments of Christ's righteousness and allow the Spirit of God to do his restorative work. When we enter in, we will find as we acknowledge, grieve, and repent that we are following the verbs of the kingdom of God. We will be compelled to go, tell, and baptize through the actions of the Spirit of God. Thank goodness we're just along for the ride.

These are all small actions: to tend a garden we did not plant, to feed sheep we have not created or sustained, to help people imagine how the guardrails Jesus puts up are good and for our flourishing.

We are witnesses. He has given us good work to do and he will do it.

• • •

Lord God, it takes much courage to consent to being restored. I know my own heart—how I tend to create my own purpose and build my own name. I desire a wholeness in my work, in my family, in my place, that is born from the spacious love of Jesus.

I open my heart now to you, O Spirit of God. Blow in and refresh me. Make Jesus bigger than my own fears or comfort. Create in me a new heart. Amen.

13

DRAWING CATHEDRALS

An Invitation to Seeing Anew

*t*he other day, prompted I'm not sure by what, I reread a story that made me cry in college: "Cathedral," by Raymond Carver. The narrator, a middle-aged man burned out and wearied by life, is annoyed by an old friend of his wife's, Robert, coming to stay the night. Robert, who's blind, has just lost his wife.

When Robert comes, the narrator tries to placate his wife, but finds the blind man pathetic. His wife can't stop smiling. She's anxious to hear about his life. Robert seems an object of pity, something to be tossed aside like their old couch, so, he wonders, how can his wife fawn over him?

Later, after his wife has gone to bed, the narrator and Robert share a smoke and flip through channels. The narrator doesn't want to be left alone with the blind man—it's as if his not seeing will expose all the unseen parts of himself.

A documentary on cathedrals comes on. Whereas before the blind man could hear a sports program and follow along, this sort of program requires more: sight. The narrator tries to describe what he's seeing on the television, but it doesn't work. It's not only that it's a hard task; it's that a cathedral doesn't mean anything. He doesn't believe in God, wouldn't know how to get something called faith. So Robert asks him to get heavy paper; they'll draw a cathedral together.

Robert's hand grips the narrator's. With encouragement, they get started and then keep going. "I put in windows with arches. I drew flying buttresses. I hung great doors. I couldn't stop. The TV station went off the air. I put down the pen and closed and opened my fingers. The blind man felt around over the paper. He moved the tips of his fingers over the paper, all over what I had drawn, and he nodded." Robert tells him to close his eyes. They keep drawing. Then, the cathedral is completed. Robert tells him to take a look. The narrator keeps his eyes closed. The story ends: "I was in my house. I knew that. But I didn't feel like I was inside anything. 'It's really something,' I said."

A German philosopher writes that our "exasperation" with the way the world works "has its roots not in what is still denied to us, but in what we have lost because we now have it under control." We have enacted liturgies of hurry and hustle to try to engineer outcomes: happiness, success, meaning. This is the sort of flat life in the immanent frame that the narrator of "Cathedral" operates in; it's our world too. We have lost resonance, the unpredictability and unengineerability of things like sleep, falling snow, the magic of late afternoon light, so much so that we've lost language for things like grace and transcendence, things we might find in a cathedral. We find ourselves trying to find a more spacious life precisely through methodologies that cannot get us there.

We need the surprising hope of resurrection. We need to be acted upon, for transcendence to break through, we need the sense of *I was in my house but I didn't feel like I was inside anything.*

When we walk into a cathedral, we can't help but shut our mouth and stare: our lips part in wonder and our eyes follow the walls all the way up to the ceiling. With chin jutting upwards, we feel our own smallness. Yet being a part of something so immense, our own internal landscape grows too. We might find ourselves asking different questions or welcomed into a spaciousness we didn't know we were longing for.

As we consider how a spaciousness can open up inside our souls, our lives may look quite plain, yet there is a growing internal cathedral that allows us space to look up and worship in whatever circumstance we find ourselves. This is the space the psalmist speaks of as having "calmed and quieted my soul, like a weaned child" (Ps 131:2). It is what Paul speaks about when he says he's learned the secret of being content in want and in plenty. It is a still spot in a frenzied world.

> The way of Jesus is not the way the world works, through hustle and hurry. It is something dramatically new.

The way of Jesus is not the way the world works, through hustle and hurry. It is something dramatically new.

• • •

When Jesus laid out his Great Commission for his disciples, after he rose from the dead, it was not so his followers could just hurry up and get after it. It was an invitation to participate in the rich, storied, and layered heart of God for the world.

Soon after Jesus gave them their work to do, he left: Jesus ascended to heaven. Right before he did, his disciples asked: "Is now the time that the kingdom will be restored?" Jesus helped them remember their limits: "It is not for you to know times or seasons that the Father has fixed by his own authority. But you will receive power when the Holy Spirit has come upon you, and you will be my witnesses in Jerusalem and in all Judea and Samaria, and to the end of the earth" (Acts 1:7-8). Faithfulness in God's commission is not gained by knowing all things; instead, our work in the world is only possible through the animation of the Spirit, the comforter and teacher Jesus promised to send. This is how Jesus is with us, even to the end of the age, through the power of the Spirit.

We cannot engineer our lives or our Christian calling and vocation. Like sleep or the gift of new falling snow, we must be drawn into something outside of ourselves, into something more beautiful and spacious.

A spacious life only comes to the extent that we cede control—letting the Spirit guide our hands and draw the cathedral of our lives himself.

The path to the spacious life doesn't simply lead to a some-day heaven, it leads to Jesus—the one who sees you, knows you, gave himself for you, forgives you, restores and reconciles you, and who sends you out with good work to do as you participate in the unlimited love of God.

The spacious place you're looking for | The spacious place
isn't only for a later time or place; it is | is God himself.
available right now. The spacious place
is God himself. And by his Spirit, he lives inside of you.

We are welcomed into the very life of the Trinity, into the dance of the triune God where all love, desire, and need are abundantly met. James B. Torrance says it like this:

> This unique relationship between Jesus and the Father is interpreted in terms of the Holy Spirit. Jesus is conceived by the Spirit, baptized by the Spirit, led by the Spirit into the wilderness. Through the eternal Spirit he offers himself to the Father on the cross and is raised from the dead by the Spirit. He receives the Spirit from the Father for us, vicariously, in his humanity, and that out of his fullness he might baptize the church by the Spirit of Pentecost into a life of shared communion, mission, and service.

You are the temple of the Holy Spirit, the cathedral and home for God himself.

• • •

In Acts 2, Luke writes that in an upper room a "violent rushing wind" came from heaven. The disciples were all gathered to-gether, afraid of the fallout when the authorities found Jesus alive. Jesus had gone back to God and left them with a mission they had no idea how to follow.

But then: It sounded like a freight train and tornado, something powerful and frightening, the wind of God rushing in. Then they saw "tongues like flames of fire that separated and rested on each one of them" (Acts 2:3 CSB). The words of the prophet Joel were in fire and wind: the Spirit was poured out, sons and daughters prophesied, creation itself changed, salvation had come down.

Peter stood up to testify to this new thing, how the crucified Jesus was Lord, how what leaders and authorities meant for evil, God used for good. The pouring out of the Spirit that day was sign and seal of the promise come true: Jesus is God, his death and resurrection rescues and redeems his people, the great day of the Lord will come, and Jesus is both Lord and Messiah!

Good news requires a response. The people heard this mighty rushing wind and the cracks in their hearts cried out for water. But how would they get this new life? They asked Peter: "What do we do?" Peter pointed out the entrance into the spacious life: "Repent and be baptized."

And then their lives changed: they gathered, they worshiped, they prayed. They lived openhanded, generous lives: they broke bread, they provided for those in need, they enjoyed the favor of all the people. They lived lives deeply connected to one another for the common good and committed to a people and a place. It is only the Spirit of God who can effect such change. More and more joined their number.

Members of one body, they were built into a house. The spacious life is contagious.

• • •

My favorite walks are not the walks to clear my head or settle down my frayed nerves; they are walks with my sister-in-law, Kerry. Through miles of terrain we have listened together about what God has done, is doing, and will do. In one walk in particular in a nature preserve with paths that wound around some plastic playground equipment, we spoke of following Jesus like the birds flitting around us.

We were being invited into flight, tucked deep under the wings of our soaring God, who shelters us there. Following Jesus' mission meant having eyes to see where he was actually flying, paying attention to where he was going, not asking God to be a genie who blesses our plan built on hustle. A more spacious life would look like staying close to his beating heart, his mothering wings, and moving in the winds he told his offspring to go. It would feel secure and exhilarating and free of the pressure to perform to be loved, because we already had it, tucked as we were under his wing.

What if the good life has nothing to do with what we try to control but everything to do with God's small invitations to name our limits, feel our humanity, and hide ourselves in him?

When we are tucked up under the wing of God, our limits can actually lead to our flourishing and the flourishing of our places. We participate in the mission; we do not command it. We simply testify to the goodness of God: we go, we tell, and when people repent, we invite them into the covenant community through baptism. We invite people into a spacious life.

It's an ordinary business. It involves all that we are, in each place that we are, doing whatever we are doing. It isn't just something for clergy or those with a fancy social media following. Steven Garber reminds us it's a way of seeing: "ordinary people that we are, living in the ordinary places that are ours, called to see all of life sacramentally, understanding our vocations as signposts for a more coherent world where things that are real and true and right are woven into the fabric of the world—eating and drinking, worshiping and working, loving and living—seamlessly connecting the world that is with the world that someday will be."

However God has made you, wherever God has placed you, with the limits that are yours to embrace, you get to be a part of his great mission: finding ways to connect the ordinary with the story of God. That is your job: to bear witness, from the budget-doing, to the carpooling, to working to end injustice, to your work and leisure. All of it is holy. All of it can be redeemed, multiplied, and given in love—from the cup of cold water given to the prayers prayed.

We are being called to be a people. We are being built into a house.

• • •

So I invite you along with me to see anew what this good and bounteous spacious life might look like.

In my mind's eye, it is springtime. The earth has begun to thaw a bit and the green is that luminescent shade of new, eager growth. The neighborhood comes alive after the solitariness of winter.

The streets are blocked off and there are vendors offering food and pretty wares. There are local bands set up on porches: a drum kit and guitarist vie for space and a vocalist finds a spot to squeeze himself into on the wrought iron. Passersby stroll through, eating their tacos or ice cream, drinking their mint lemonade and iced coffees. They stop, smile and watch, letting the music wash over them.

Then they walk to the next home. More bands are set up in the neighborhood, playing different tunes. Audience and musicians smile together at a world they both participate in: sunshine and music, sugary fingers and calloused hands, creating beauty in a shared moment. Someone on another porch is reading a poem, another home offers a story for children. Maybe someone plays a trumpet in the grass or picks a fiddle.

As I imagine it, the streets are free of cars. There's a long table with pure white linens set up right in the middle of the street. It goes on and on and on. Vines tumble from the edges and the sun glints off silver cutlery. Candles fill it to overflowing, orchids arch their necks. And there is a place for everyone to sit down.

When God invited you into a more spacious life as you found yourself burdened by comparison and bent down by hustle and hurry, the invitation seemed more than you'd dreamed. But then you walked into this house God had made and felt a bit cramped. You walked through temptation and suffering, pain and injustice. You were invited to wrestle with God, to see the ancient pathways as the good paths to human flourishing.

When the invitation felt claustrophobic and dark, you found you had a man of sorrows there with you, one who had also been betrayed and felt alone. You found perhaps an easy chair, a blanket, and a small flicker of light in those dark places in your soul, showing you that you didn't need to be afraid. There was a place for you too.

Then he took you and turned on the lights and led you out from those dark corners, and suddenly, the cramped spaces—your very losses and limits—were transformed. What was loss turned out to be gift. What was death turned out to be life. All of it is invitation.

He has you still.

You feel that pulse of being safe and known as he is leading you out, right to where you began, to the entrance to the house, to be (like him) the inviting one. More and more people need the weight of hustle and hurry lifted from their shoulders. You know someone who needs the transcendent to break in through a kind word, a small gift, a prayer offered, or even a hard question. You know how you could put your arm around another hurting one or have them put their arms around you. You see the possibilities, the vistas expand.

He has brought you from the small, dark corners back to the entrance of the house. You peer out. There's music and you're a bit unsure about what to do—now that you've let go of how you thought life should be by ceding control, after you've let go of choosing to blame other people and God for pain or sin or brokenness. Now that you've been exposed and wrestled with God and found he has never let you go.

He brings the Comforter alongside to guide and direct, he wraps you in his blanket of love, and he lets you peer out the front door.

You could find your people here, those who have entered into this spacious narrow way. They look a bit ragged like you, but they also look lovely—making music together. You love how it all sounds, how each one is unique, playing their own lines, but together it sounds fresh and new.

You are being invited and sent on mission: into the depths of the spacious life. To bring more people in to a life with limits, lived under the loving care of a Shepherd King.

He has your hand under his, drawing the lines of your life like the lines of a cathedral.

The tables are set. There's a party on the porch. The doorway is open. Jesus has gone ahead of us. He calls us to follow. Let's give it a go. Welcome home, friend. Here is a more spacious life.

• • •

Spirit, enliven me. Give me the grace to participate in the mission of God through small and ordinary things. Prick my ears and open my eyes. Assure me of the presence and glory of Jesus. Draw my life into a cathedral for your glory. Bit by bit, line by line, I am yours. Open my eyes to the glory of knowing you. Amen.

ACKNOWLEDGMENTS

i wrote this book when my time grew increasingly limited. The generosity of publishers, editors, other writers, and family surrounded me. They walked me through dark seasons, named my limits with me—and did so with hope.

Thank you to Don Gates and InterVarsity Press for finding this book a home, cheering it on, and helping bring it to print. Particular thanks to Elissa Schauer who helped birth this book alongside me. The rest of the editorial, marketing, and sales teams were wonderful to work with.

All good books come from conversation. Thanks go to Redbud Writers Guild who helped me with title and subtitle ideas, encouragement, and writerly camaraderie. Thank you to editors at *Christianity Today*, *inTouch Magazine*, and other places around the web for giving me space to work out some of these ideas.

Finding friends and colleagues is a joy alongside the solitary life of writing. Big thanks go to Jen, Laura, Cara, Lore, K. J., Meredith, Summer, and Brandon, particularly for your good questions and encouragement. Thank you to Marlena for reading a draft of earlier chapters and to Anjuli for your language of invitation. Thank you to friends near and far: Melissa, Kirstie, Alita, Jen, Jeff, and Jackie, who pressed in and prayed for us. Thank you to Jill Sweet for listening to the Spirit with me. Thank you to Ken and Tammie for your deep faithfulness in prayer, your friendship and snark. You are treasures.

A big thank you goes to my guests on the *Finding Holy* podcast—thank you for creating a kind, collegial space of welcome and good questions.

This book would not have come to print without dear friends offering a spacious place for us. Thank you to Jason and Karla, for offering friendship and your very lives these last several years. I do not seem to be able to find the right words to thank you and to express my deep gratitude. We love you and will always hold the mountains with us.

Thank you to Ken and Gillian, friends who will bear with my big questions and serve us feasts around tables. You have created for us spacious places to rest, to be listened to, to dream, and to be reminded in bread and wine of the good story of the gospel. Thank you.

Thank you to Kerry and Carter, for your example of faithfulness, of pressing into Jesus, and for watching to see where God is at work around the world. Thank you for walks and conversations and for loving our children too. We love you.

Thank you to Howard and Roberta, for providing a literal spacious place for us to rest in this season, and for gorgeous meals and conversation. All of life is lit by flame, there is glory when we look. Your hospitality is pure delight, your friendship a treasure.

Thank you to my parents, Tor and Carolyn, and my in-laws, John and Sally, for the ways you have fed us, cared for us, welcomed us, and loved us. We couldn't do it without you.

My deepest limits are felt of course by those closest to me. I'm thankful to my husband and four children for the ways you see my limits and love me still. You are testaments to grace. Ezra, may you always trust in the unlimited rightness of Jesus as the foundation for your life. Porter, may the Spirit comfort you and may you always do your work with joy. Camden, may you find the goodness of Jesus to be the beauty you hold on to. Harriet, may your joy be full in how Jesus calls you his beloved.

This book would not have come to be without Bryce, who limits himself for the sake of love. You make love look beautiful, and because I am loved by you, I want more of Jesus. You are my greatest gift and treasure.

Jesus, thank you for being my kind and good shepherd, the house I am learning to be most fully at home in. That you would give me your attention is gift and life itself. May this small book be a witness and memorial stone, something like a seed that you would cause to grow as you see fit.

And my dear reader, I pray you would find a home in these words so that you might find a home in the Word. It's spacious there.

DISCUSSION QUESTIONS

1. Where has your life been characterized by hustle and hurry, or where have you seen it in your cultural context?

2. What is your response to this idea: "Limits are built into the fabric of creation as part of God's loving rule and care. Limits are not a result of sin, strictures to hold us down, but a part of God's very good plan" (14)?

3. How has "digital everywhere-ism" infected your life? What guardrails might you put up around technology use so you can be present in your body, place, and time?

4. Ashley writes about how waiting well looks like naming "the shape of our pain" and lament (40-41). What emotions does waiting bring up for you? Work together to reframe these uncomfortable feelings as an invitation to know God. If waiting makes you feel out of control and that makes you anxious, meditate on God's control, his faithfulness, and his nearness to you.

5. How do you react to your limitations: Do you tend to blame others, fall into shame, try to control them, fight, or ignore them? What might be Jesus' invitation to you instead?

6. In the discussion of sleep and Sabbath, Ashley writes that we can "live in time like a place" (54-55). How would your time, calendar, and priorities look different if they had this sense of spaciousness? What's a small step to get you started?

7. Ashley reminds us that "our noes make room for the right yeses" (59). What is your first reaction to this invitation? What might God be asking you to say no to so you have room for the right yes?

8. "Play is an act of protest against value and worth being measured by what we produce" (67). Do you play? How might you practice play and delight?

9. "Rich community in the church . . . builds and grows in its flavor only through constraints" (87). What constraints do you experience in community? How might each be a gift? Where have you noticed others constraining themselves to love you?

10. Ashley reminds us that the root of *abide* is to stay put, watch, and wait defiantly (103). Where have you experienced the abiding presence of another? How has Christ abode with you? What might it look like to abide in Christ in your weekly schedule?

11. We often conceive of freedom as freedom from constraints, but what if it's not simply freedom *from* but also freedom *for*? "For freedom Christ has set us free" (Gal 5:1). What has Jesus set you free from, and what has he set you free for?

12. Ashley asks if we're more concerned about achieving something for ourselves than about participating in the kingdom of God (131). What's the difference between these two? How might your limits be a light on the dashboard of your life warning you to look beneath the surface?

13. "Good news requires a response" (138). As you've read, have you experienced a sense of internal spaciousness? What response might you want to enact to God's invitation to name your limits as part of knowing him?

14. "Jesus is the spacious place itself" (109). How have you experienced this?

15. Which invitation in the book do you most desire to practice? How might you do that? How might your group or community take an invitation and practice it together?

NOTES

1 THE SUPERMARKET OF LIFE

2 *The gap between my imagined life and my given one:* Wendell Berry writes, "We live the given life, and not the planned," in *A Timbered Choir: The Sabbath Poems 1979–1997* (Washington, DC: Counterpoint, 1998), 178.

4 *Experiment in crafting:* Ada Calhoun, *Why We Can't Sleep: Women's New Midlife Crisis* (New York: Grove, 2020), introduction, ebook edition.

5 *In a culture of "I'm Free to Be Myself":* David Brooks, *The Second Mountain: The Quest for a Moral Life* (New York: Random House, 2019), 13.

8 *If the kingdom of heaven is at hand:* Fleming Rutledge, *Advent: The Once and Future Coming of Jesus Christ* (Grand Rapids, MI: Eerdmans, 2018), 324.

9 *True freedom is not found:* Lesslie Newbigin, *Foolishness to the Greeks: The Gospel and Western Culture* (Grand Rapids, MI : Eerdmans, 1986), 119.

10 *The loss of guardrails:* James K. A. Smith, *On the Road with St. Augustine: A Real-World Spirituality for Restless Hearts* (Grand Rapids, MI: Brazos, 2019), 62-63.

2 AND LIMITS WERE GOOD, VERY GOOD

16 *It was our sorry case:* St. Athanasius, "On the Incarnation," Copticchurch.net, www.copticchurch.net/topics/theology/incarnation_st_athanasius.pdf, 8.

20 *live for the life of the world:* This phrase comes from Alexander Schmemann, *For the Life of the World: Sacraments and Orthodoxy* (Crestwood, NY: St. Vladimir's Seminary Press, 2004).

3 JESUS ISN'T ON INSTAGRAM

25 *Recent study with "hard-core gamers":* Michael Brendan Dougherty, "A Conspiracy Theory Worth Considering," *National Review*, January 13, 2021, www.nationalreview.com/2021/01/a-conspiracy-theory-worth -considering/.

26   *We use technology to rebel*: David Zahl, *Seculosity: How Career, Parenting, Technology, Food, Politics, and Romance Became Our New Religion and What to Do About It* (Minneapolis: Fortress, 2019), 79.

29   *Sorrow and love flow mingled down*: Isaac Watts, "When I Survey the Wondrous Cross" (1707).

30   *One wild and precious life*: Mary Oliver, "The Summer Day," www.loc .gov/poetry/180/133.html.

31   *We will have to start over*: Wendell Berry, "Faustian Economics: Hell Hath No Limits," *Harper's*, May 2008, https://harpers.org/archive /2008/05/faustian-economics/.

4 OF CUCUMBERS AND SKIPPING STONES

35   *Impatience with waiting is nothing new*: Part of this chapter was previously published in Ashley Hales, "Waiting Time Isn't Wasted Time," *Christianity Today*, April 10, 2019, www.christianitytoday.com/ct/2019 /april-web-only/delayed-response-jason-farman-art-waiting.html. Used with permission.

38   *So deep it can reach*: Frederick Dale Bruner, *Matthew: A Commentary*, vol. 1: *The Christbook* (Grand Rapids, MI: Eerdmans, 2004), 126.

40   *The shape of our pain*: Seth Haines, *The Book of Waking Up: Experiencing the Divine Love That Reorders a Life* (Grand Rapids, MI: Zondervan: 2020), 84.

41   *Walter Brueggemann writes that:* Walter Brueggemann, *Spirituality of the Psalms* (Minneapolis: Augsburg Fortress, 2002).

42   *That God is rich in mercy*: Dane Ortlund, *Gentle and Lowly: The Heart of Christ for Sinners and Sufferers* (Wheaton, IL: Crossway, 2020), 179.

5 THE SPIRITUAL LIFE IS NOT AN INSTANT POT

46   *Viral cooking appliance*: Gabriella Gersheson, "The Instant Pot Cult Is Real," *Taste Cooking*, February 8, 2017, www.tastecooking.com/instant -pot-cult-real/.

47   *Slowest form of personal transformation*: See Jill Sweet, Come Learn Rest Ministries, https://comelearnrest.com.

49   *Honey on their tongues*: A. J. Swoboda and James Bryan Smith, "Conversation with A. J. Swoboda," November 6, 2019, *in Things Above*, podcast, https://apprenticeinstitute.org/2019/11/06/conversation-with-a-j -swoboda/.

49 *A peaceful night and a perfect end*: Words of Compline, *The Book of Common Prayer (2019)* (Huntington Beach, CA: Anglican Liturgy Press, 2019).

50 *Hurry does violence to the soul*: Jefferson Bethke, *To Hell with the Hustle: Reclaiming your Life in an Overworked, Overspent and Overconnected World* (Nashville: Thomas Nelson, 2019), 94.

51 *Lord! Save! Dying!*: Frederick Dale Bruner, *Matthew: A Commentary*, vol. 1: *The Christbook* (Grand Rapids, MI: Eerdmans, 2004), 398.

   Why are you such cowards?: Bruner, *Matthew*, 398.

   The Lord in heaven neither sleeps: Bruner, *Matthew*, 398.

52 *A declaration of trust*: James Bryan Smith, *The Good and Beautiful God: Falling in Love with the God Jesus Knows* (Downers Grover, IL: Inter-Varsity Press, 2009), 34.

54 *Architecture of time*: Abraham Joshua Heschel, *The Sabbath: Its Meaning for Modern Man* (New York: Farrar, Straus and Giroux, 2005), 8, 10.

6 FLYING KITES ON THE EDGE OF THE SEA

61 *If our Lord was "the Man of Sorrows"*: B. B. Warfield, "The Emotional Life of Our Lord," available at Monergism, www.monergism.com/the threshold/articles/onsite/emotionallife.html.

62 *The supreme source of all things*: St. Augustine, *On the Trinity* 6.10, available at www.ewtn.com/catholicism/library/on-the-trinity -vviii-9097.

   Jesus, from time eternal, has been in a dance: See Scott Swain, "That Your Joy May Be Full: A Theology of Happiness," *Desiring God*, April 23, 2018, www.desiringgod.org/articles/that-your-joy-may-be-full.

63 *Play subverts this story*: Rubem Azevedo Alves, "Play or How to Subvert Dominant Values," *Union Seminary Quarterly Review* 26, no. 1 (Fall 1970): 43-57.

65 *Preserve us from faithless fears*: "For Trustfulness in Times of Worry and Anxiety," *The Book of Common Prayer (2019)* (Huntington Beach, CA: Anglican Liturgy Press, 2019), 670.

7 LOVE ISN'T A COCKTAIL PARTY

73 *Hurry and love are incompatible*: John Mark Comer, *The Ruthless Elimination of Hurry: How to Stay Emotionally Healthy and Spiritually Alive in the Chaos*

of the Modern World (New York: Crown, 2019), 23.

74 *The general human failing*: Dallas Willard, *The Spirit of the Disciplines: Understanding How God Changes Lives* (New York: HarperCollins, 1988), 6.

77 *Not only making the space but taking the time*: Malcolm Guite, *Word in the Wilderness: A Poem A Day for Lent and Easter* (London: Canterbury Press Norwich, 2014), 22.

8 THE GOODNESS OF GATHERED SALT

83 *Salt has a greater impact*: Samin Nosrat, *Salt, Fat, Acid, Heat: Mastering the Elements of Good Cooking* (New York: Simon & Schuster, 2017), 20.

The advent of the Son of God expands God's people: This idea is paraphrased from Davies and Allison in Frederick Dale Bruner, *Matthew: A Commentary*, vol. 1: *The Christbook* (Grand Rapids, MI: Eerdmans, 2004), 189.

84 *Salt has its* own *particular taste*: Nosrat, *Salt, Fat, Acid, Heat*, 21.

85 *live for the life of the world:* This phrase comes from Alexander Schmemann, *For the Life of the World: Sacraments and Orthodoxy* (Crestwood, NY: St. Vladimir's Seminary Press, 2004).

87 *In a North American context*: Seth D. Kaplan, "What is Community?," *Comment Magazine*, February 27, 2020, www.cardus.ca/comment /article/what-is-community/.

9 THE GIVENNESS OF THINGS

95 *To revel in new exploration*: Douglas McKelvey, "A Liturgy for Leaving on Holiday," *Every Moment Holy* (Nashville: Rabbit Room, 2017), 68-70.

97 *There's something about the aggregate*: Julie Beck, "What It's Like to Carry on a Tradition with a Friend Who Can't Remember It," *The Atlantic*, January 22, 2021, www.theatlantic.com/family/archive/2021/01/friends -who-high-five-every-week/617775/.

10 PRACTICING THE ART OF DYING

105 *Offered the hope that a path of life*: Laura Fabrycky, *Keys to Bonhoeffer's Haus: Exploring the World and Wisdom of Dietrich Bonhoeffer* (Minneapolis: Fortress, 2020), 188.

107 *They little know how dearly*: John Milton, *Paradise Lost*, book 4. See The John Milton Reading Room, Dartmouth College, www.dartmouth .edu/~milton/reading_room/pl/book_4/text.shtml.

11 FOLLOWING THE GUARDRAILS OF LOVE

113 *Turn off her "worry brain":* Sissy Goff, *Raising Worry-Free Girls: Helping Your Daughter Feel Braver, Stronger, and Smarter in an Anxious World* (Bloomington, MN: Bethany House, 2019), 114.

If freedom is going to be: James K. A. Smith, *On the Road with St. Augustine: A Real-World Spirituality for Restless Hearts* (Grand Rapids, MI: Brazos Press, 2019), 66.

Holy day to sit, wait, and hope: A. J. Swoboda, *A Glorious Dark: Finding Hope in the Tension Between Belief and Experience* (Grand Rapids, MI: Baker Books, 2014), 100.

116 *Grasped by what we cannot grasp:* Rainier Marie Rilke, "A Walk," trans. Robert Bly, All Poetry, https://allpoetry.com/A-Walk.

Easter was when Hope in person: N. T. Wright, *Surprised by Hope: Rethinking Heaven, the Resurrection, and the Mission of the Church* (San Francisco: HarperOne, 2008), 29.

117 *News from a country we have never yet visited:* C. S. Lewis, *The Weight of Glory: And Other Addresses* (New York: HarperCollins, 1980), 31.

118 *There was art on the walls:* The art displayed is by William Kurelek, and a copy may be found in his book, *A Northern Nativity: Christmas Dreams of a Prairie Boy.*

12 SOME SUPERHEROES CLEAN TOILETS

125 *The evidence of Christ's mercy:* Dane Ortlund, *Gentle and Lowly: The Heart of Christ for Sinners and Sufferers* (Wheaton, IL: Crossway, 2020), 179.

128 *Mothers—like fathers, like children:* Jen Pollock Michel, "Amy Coney Barrett's Message: The Maternal Hero Is a Myth," *Christianity Today*, October 16, 2020, www.christianitytoday.com/ct/2020/october-web-only/amy-coney-barrett-motherhood-message-kill-myth-hero.html.

129 *To glorify God:* The first question of *Westminster Shorter Catechism* is "What is the chief end of man?" The answer: "Man's chief end is to glorify God, and to enjoy him forever."

13 DRAWING CATHEDRALS

133 *I reread a story that made me cry:* Raymond Carver, "Cathedral," *Cathedral: Short Stories* (New York: Vintage, 1983), ebook.

134   *Exasperation . . . has its roots*: Hartmut Rosa, *The Uncontrollability of the World*, trans., James Wagner (Cambridge, UK: Polity Press, 2020) 117. His examples of snow and unengineerability come from his preface, viii.

137   *This unique relationship between Jesus and the Father*: James B. Torrance, *Worship, Community and the Triune God of Grace* (Downers Grove, IL: IVP Academic, 1996), 31.

140   *Ordinary people that we are*: Steven Garber, *The Seamless Life: A Tapestry of Love and Learning, Worship and Work* (Downers Grove, IL: Inter-Varsity Press 2020), 54.

ALSO BY ASHLEY HALES

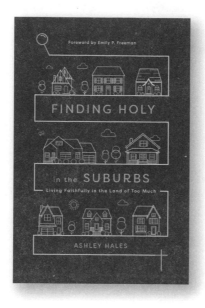